THE HOUSE OF CESSNA
BOOK I

With Commentaries

By

C. W. Cissna

A reprint of the 1901 research by Howard Cessna, with commentaries that reflect new research.

Privately Published
Albuquerque, NM
September 2011

COMMENTARY:

This volume is a digital scan; of a 30 year old photo copy; of a 50 year old micro film; of a 30 year old copy of Howard Cessna's book published in 1901. It had a very limited printing and it has been difficult for most people to get a copy. In the text, he states that it is his wish for future generations to use this material to continue their historical search. Every member of this great family owes an enormous debt of gratitude for his work and sacrifice. He was the first of our family's historians.

That being said, there are qualifications to be made to his work. Hence comes the writing of the commentary version. Travel and research were very difficult in the late 1800's. Our century has afforded many more opportunities for uncover facts. Local Historical Societies have produced indexes of land, court, marriage, death, cemetery and other records. Many long lost books have been digitized by Google and it is possible to look in places that Howard Cessna did not have access to.

Commentary pages have been inserted along with his original work to point researchers in a clearer direction. No criticism is intended of our benefactor, Howard Cessna. We all start with his work, and pursue a clearer understanding of history.

NOTE: Several pages of his book have been omitted. They were of photos that were so badly faded as to be unrecognizable. To save printing costs these were not included.

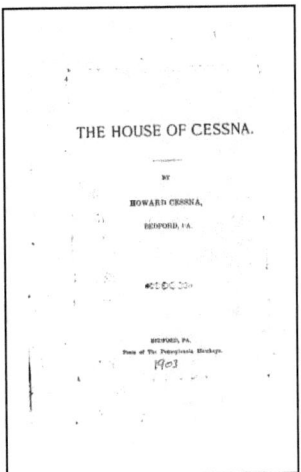

THE HOUSE OF CESSNA.

BY

HOWARD CESSNA,

BEDFORD, PA.

BEDFORD, PA.
Press of The Pennsylvania Herald.
1903

4

Contents as follows:

5

Pictures.

COMMENTARY: Caution about Records

Family historians who research should use caution about what they accept as fact. It is always wise to find the oldest records possible and view them.   Taking the work of others at face value can be dangerous.

For example: in 1990, I completed a booklet for our immediate family. It was hurried and incomplete because we were preparing it for a Family Reunion and additions would be made at the gathering.   Although only 50 copies were printed (for family consumption only), one person released it to the Church of Latter Day Saints genealogy department.   It has since been published widely, and it was recently discovered for sale on the internet.

The problem is that it is FULL of errors.   It was never intended to be a scholarly research work, only a family souvenir.   A corrected edition will be published in the months ahead.

The Church of LDS has provided a tremendous gift to researchers by making records available.   However, please remember the group's reasons for research are not the same as yours.   They do not have a need to collect death data. Nor are they as concerned with accuracy as you will want to be.   They merely publish information that is given to them, and do not check for accuracy. Use their work to find a direction for your search, not as an authority for facts.

Another caution is researchers should always cross reference data with what else was going on in history. It is inspiring that the family migration across this country mirrors the time that land was opened for settlement. Cessna/Cissna's were among the first of every generation of pioneers in almost every region of the country.

HOWARD CESSNA.

Howard Cessna, Esq., was born at the Cessna homestead in Colerain township, Bedford County, Penna., October 27, 1870. He received his early education in the public schools; taught school in Southampton township and also in the Clifton Masonic Academy in Wayne County, Tennessee. He returned North to complete his education at the Millersville State Normal School, from which institution he graduated in 1892. After graduating he taught another term of school in Bedford County, this time as Principal of the Mann's Choice schools. He then entered the office of his uncle, the late Hon. John Cessna, to study law. After careful preparation he was admitted to the Bar of Bedford County, on October 6, 1894. The following year he practiced law at Bedford. On the 18th day of September, 1895, he located at Everett, Penna. After locating at Everett he labored diligently to build up a successful practice, acquiring a reputation for ability and sterling honesty and made many friends and admirers regardless of political affiliation. As a public speaker he stands prominent among the young men of Bedford County, having made numerous political and patriotic speeches at home and abroad.

In the spring of 1902 he returned to Bedford where he again resumed the practice of law, devoting considerable of his time to disposing of 7,000 acres of his real estate which he recently sold to the State.

The reader will note the time and work required of him in the preparation of such a work as this and all members of the House of Cessna are certainly much indebted to him for the completion of this book.

HARRY CESSNA.

HOWARD CESSNA.
Pages IX and 3.

AUTHOR'S PREFACE.

BEDFORD, PA., March 7, 1903.

At least ten years ago the writer began this work. Believing the time at hand for any effort that might be made to preserve the history of the Cessnas in America, I first obtained a statement from Hon. John Cessna, of Bedford, concerning his knowledge of the early Cessnas. Later Henry Hemming, whose mother was a Cessna, at the age of 80, with a mind clear as a bell, added greatly to what my uncle gave. Innumerable letters were exchanged with Cessnas all over the Union. Many expressing the greatest delight to assist in giving all information at their command.

It is a pity that some one did not begin the work a couple decades earlier as absolute accuracy could then have followed. Had Jonathan Cessna IV. (d. 1853) or Squire Jim Cessna IV. been consulted in an effort of this kind valuable data would have been obtained. But believing that better late than never, I continued as best I could. If complaining would accomplish anything I should have just cause against the many that indifferently treated my correspondence, though I am told the same spirit is universally shown in all such movements. Among the more willing descendants to aid me, I desire to mention the names of the following: Dr. J. P. Cessna, Canfield, O.; John M. Sears, Salem, O.; G. E. Cessna, Bowlingreen, O.; Wm. Cessna Durham, Hodgensville, Ky.; John Cessna, Elderton, Pa.; Geo. W. Cisney, Carlisle, Pa.; W. A. Cisne, Iowa City, Ia.; John R. Cessna, Bladensburg, O.; Mrs. Kate (Cisne) Walters, Fairfield, Ill., and last, but not least, J. Wilson Cessna, of Nevada, Ia. Scores of others have aided me materially.

There will appear errors in this work which can be corrected by parties discovering such, addressing a letter to me which, together with copy of book, all letters received, and any additional knowledge will be filed in the Court

11

House vault here at Bedford, Pa., in care of Bedford County Historical Association.

It is the intention to later in life revise this work and include therein the History of the Cessna family in France. There is not the slightest doubt that the Cessnas belong to the Nobility of France. In English Histories John Cessna I. is styled Count. Had the preparation of this work effected less my attention to my profession, I intended to complete the task including the Cessnas of France in this effort.

In the event of death preventing my revising this work any descendant of John Cessna I. desiring to continue the work will find all letters, papers, etc., received by me in care of said Historical Society.

There is no purpose to make money by publishing this work. Any profit will be spent in erecting a marker over the grave of Maj. John Cessna III. as well as locating the field where John Cessna II. was captured by the Indians. It may not be improper to here mention the seeming neglect shown the graves of Cessnas nearer than three or four generations. Remember America is practically a new country and a little care along this line now will live for ages.

The reader will observe many different ways in which our name is spelled. Such a peculiarity is prominent among all the old names here in the east. I have noticed in genealogical works as high as fourteen changes in orthography. This can partly be accounted for by reason of the early clerks, assessors, etc., knowing best but one language and spelling by guess unfamiliar names of immigrants from countries other than their own. From what I learn it looks as if all of us have dropped the original way of spelling our name. De Cessna seems to be the way it was spelled in France, though in the Congressional Library at Washington in a Dictionary of Biographical names, I find where a journalist by the name of A. G. Cesena died at Beaujen, France, in 1815. The following changes in orthography will be noted: De Cessna, Cesena, Cessna, Cissna, Cisna, Cisne, Cisney and Sisney—all descendants of John Cessna I. I do not propose to defend the spelling of any way but desire

12

calling attention to the fact that Col Charles Cessna III. in his papers filed at Harrisburg used Cessna. Judging from his writing and reports filed during the Revolutionary War he was precise and scholarly.

The omission of pictures and list of descendants—if there be any—must not be blamed on the author as he has been more than willing to use all data obtained.

From letters on file I learn that in religion the Cessnas belong to a score or more of protestant denominations; that the name has been represented in every military conflict from 1750 to the present; and that in politics active advocates for both the leading parties in the past and present— were among the Cessnas.

The absence of any hereditary disease among the Cessnas can best be noted when we observe its devastation in other families. The strong constitution and physique of the older Cessnas will largely be retained in the House of Cessna by marriage to those free from hereditary weakness. In this age of literature, the coming generations find a foe in the world's field of competition better equipped with an education than the rivals of our ancestors. To see, however, that the children are educated is the surest and most permanent means of adding glory to our name.

IMPORTANCE OF PRESERVING RECORDS.

The importance of preserving records is graphically set forth in the following article prepared by the Historical Society of Philadelphia.

It is the misfortune of the nations of the old continent, that their early history is lost in the night of time. Excepting the Holy Scriptures, no records have been preserved of the first settlements of mankind. All else beyond a period not very remote is veiled in obscurity. Recourse has been had to fabulous traditions made up of fabled heroes and demi-gods in abundance, the offspring of vanity and of ignorance. Of our British ancestors, nothing is known before the invasions of their island by Julius Caesar; of our German forefathers, the noble defense made by the immortal Herman against the legions of Varns, whom he defeated and conquerred, is the first authentic account after which follows a long period of darkness to the time of their great Emperor Charlemagne. The ancient history of Asia (the cradle of mankind) engages at this moment the attention of the learners of Europe. For that purpose, Asiatic societies have been formed under royal patronage, both in England and in France. The study of Egyptian antiquities is everywhere patronized, encouraged, and promoted. Scientific travelers are sent to that country at royal expense, obelisks and other monuments are imported at an immense cost, and grace the public squares, museums, and other repositories of the great capitols. England boasts of the rosetta monumental stone, France of her Egyptian obelisk, which once adorned ancient Thebes, and is now erected in the midst of her capitol, where it is the most attractive object to the admiration of travelers.

Unable to penetrate into the future, man loves to inquire into the past to interrogate his most remote ancestors,

and to learn from their experience how to pursue good and
eschew evil. He is disappointed and mortified, when instead of historical facts, he. finds fabulous records and in-
credible tales, more calculated for the amusement of children than the instruction of mankind."

To avoid fabulous records so far as the Cessnas of
America are concerned is one of the objects of this work.

Story of the Huguenots.

In order that the reader may refresh his memory as to French History, a gist is here given of Rev. A. Stapleton's "Memorials of The Huguenots"—a book recently compiled and the first of its kind ever published. Any reader desiring a copy should address Rev. Stapleton, Carlisle, Pa.

"In the study of French History we learn that in 1517 Martin Luther started a movement against the Catholic Church. As the feeling against the church grew, it was necessary for the anti-Catholics or Reformers to have their own pastors and leaders, hence they organized and in France such Reformers were called Huguenots. The feeling against the church grew rapidly when in 1525 a Huguenot entered Catholic churches, broke the images and posted placards denouncing the corruptions of the Pope and church. For this he was burned at the stake. From this time until 1560 the Huguenots were severely persecuted, when the Papists (Catholics) and Huguenots came together on the field of battle, resulting in the massacre of 12,000 Huguenot prisoners. Complications with foreign countries ameliorated matters for awhile during which time the religious trouble was debated in public by each side sending its foremost advocate as a representative. The Huguenot theologian "with nothing but the Bible as his text-book completely swept away the Romish traditions and dogmas of the cardinal." From results of debate it was thought liberal religious toleration would follow but the Catholic leaders would not permit such. So when about 1200 Huguenots, who were engaged in worship, had assembled the most of them were massacred in a most horrible manner. A Catholic leader attempting to defend the action of those taking part in this slaughter, was answered by language that has become historic: "Sir, it certainly becomes the church of God in whose cause I speak, to endure blows, and not strike them; but may it please your majesty also to remember that it is an anvil which has worn out many a hammer."

War between the two factions followed, the Catholics being aided by soldiers from Spain and the Huguenots from the Protestants of Germany. A victory on the part of the Protstants would be followed by a treaty, which lasted only long enough to permit Catholics to acquire advantage by deception. In violation of promises 10,000 Huguenots were killed in the most horrible manner in less than three months.

In 1569 when engaged in battle the Huguenots lost two-thirds of their men, but immediately reorganized the army and in the following year were so successful as to obtain a treaty that gave them more freedom.

"The verdict of history is that the Papacy never surrenders to a dissenter the right of conscience, hence what cannot be done by force must be done by intrigue and assassination." Therefore the Catholic leaders to deceive, feigned the greatest friendship for the Huguenots. When the Protestant leaders accepted their invitations some were poisoned and others assassinated.

"On Sunday morning, St. Bartholomew's Day, Aug. 24, 1572, a signal was given by the tolling of the great bell just after midnight and the number of Huguenots massacred in the city of Paris is estimated at from 3,000 to 10,000. Orders were issued then to other cities of France to purge themselves in like manner of heretics. The entire Huguenot victims killed throughout the country was probably between 20,000 and 30,000. This movement is so horrible that history fails to tell of another its equal. Let it be erased from the memory of man."

It is claimed by some that this massacre was ordered to offset a move contemplated by Huguenots against the Royal Family and that the Pope's great delight in hearing of so many Huguenots being killed, was due to a supposed plot being thereby thwarted against the Catholic Church.

Instead of such methods crushing out the movement of the Reformation it only served to rouse the Huguenots to a more determined defence of their faith. The following seventeen years was but turmoil for France.

The Catholics became jealous of their leaders and a Monk stabbed the King whose successor was a Protestant. As the Catholics were in the majority, he could hold the throne only by force. The Huguenots, aided by Queen Elizabeth of England, defended him, and King Philip II., of Spain, aided the Catholics. This war lasted four years, during which time the noted battle of Ivey was fought when the King himself (Henry of Bourbon) led the Huguenots to victory after telling them to follow the white plume of his hat. Strange to relate the King ended this war by himself becoming a Catholic. Doubtless his motive was of a two-fold purpose as he later secured great freedom for the Huguenots and issued the edict of Nantes, April 15, 1598. This gave the Protestants practically freedom of worship, opened to them all political offices and employment, and gave them as places of refuge a large number of fortified towns

The Protestants got along reasonably well until a Jesuit assassinated King Henry because of his religious toleration. A veritable reign of terror prevailed and about 1629 the Huguenots after many attempts practically gave up armed resistance. Immediately innumerable plans to force and secure Protestants to join the Catholic faith followed. Some were purchased, churches were destroyed, preachers limited as to what to discuss in public, and finally the King's soldiers were placed among the Huguenots to support. The privacy of the home was broken up, all valuables were taken and depredations of all kind were committed. The Protestants were debarred from holding public office and were virtually deprived of all civil rights.

Converts to Catholicism were given three years grace for the payment of debts, were exempted from paying tax and military duty. Frequently at the point of the bayonet the Huguenots were forced to destroy their own churches. Thousands sought relief by flight which the authorities sought to prevent but in vain. By official proclamation England, Holland, Switzerland and Denmark offered asylum to the refugees. Many of the nobles and literary men who had escaped to foreign lands exerted a powerful influence in their adopted countries in behalf of their oppressed countrymen. The King continued to turn a deaf ear to all entreaties and on October 18, 1865, signed the Revocation of the Edict of Nantes. This made it unlawful to exercise in the Protestant religion. Pastors were ordered to leave the country. Parents were compelled to have the priests baptize and instruct their children. They were forbidden to emigrate and those who had done so must return in four months or suffer the confiscation of their property. (It was at this period John Cessna I. left France.) About 1200 of the nobility together with possibly a million other citizens left France. From twelve to thirteen hundred refugees were seen to pass Geneva, in Switzerland' in a week. Their plan of escape was similar to the underground railroad system in this country. Many refugees entered the military service of other lands. England alone organized eleven regiments of Huguenot soldiers and one brigade under Duke De Schomburg fought under Prince of Orange at the battle of the Boyne in Ireland 1690. Count John De Cessna was in this brigade as an officer.

There is perhaps no people in Europe less disposed to emigrate than the French. They are naturally much attached to their country. No great mass of French are found in the United States as is the case with other European nationalities. Both Catholics and Protestants alike now delight to stay in their own sunny clime where they can worship God as their conscience dictates. * * * * *

There is perhaps no aspect of the history of the Huguenots in America that impress the historian more profoundly than the record of their public service. Pennsylvania alone furnished in the Revolution Elias Bondinot a President and

19

Michael Hillegas the first Treasurer of the Nation; Major General Daniel Roberdean and Brigadier General Philip de Haas. Besides the foregoing the Pennsylvania Huguenots furnished fifteen colonels for the Revolution besides a proportionate number of officers of lesser rank. Among these fifteen colonels appear the names of Col. John Cessna and his brother, Col. Charles Cessna.

This same preponderating prominence is shown in other lines of public service of which we will only name the Judiciary of Pennsylvania. We may note Judge S. Leslie Mestrezat of the Supreme, and Ex-Governor James A. Beaver of the Superior Court; Judge Cyrus L. Pershing, Judge J. W. Bittenger, Judge Dimmer Beeber, and Judge de Pew La Bar.

Among some of the more prominent descendants of Huguenots in America are Admiral Winfield Scott Schley, Chief Justice Jay, President Tyler, Garfield, Roosevelt, Alexander Hamilton, the Bayards of Delaware, Commodore Stephen Decatur, Admiral George Dewey, and the poet Whittier.

In Rev. Stapleton's "Memorials of the Huguenots" appears the following:

De Cessna—Among the heroes of the Duke De Schomburg at the battle of the Boyne (1690) was a young Huguenot soldier Jean De Cessna who remained in Ireland after the forces of William, Prince of Orange, were withdrawn. In 1718 he came to Pennsylvania and located in Lancaster County. (1.) Later he removed to York County where he died in 1751. (2.) Several of his sons located in Shippensburg as early as 1751 and then later removed to Bedford County where the family became prominent. John De Cessna (1718-1800) of Bedford County, was one of the leading men of the Province. He was a member of the Provincial Assembly and Constitutional Convention of 1775 and a colonel in the Revolutionary War. His brother, Charles De Cessna, was likewise a colonel in the War of Independence. The late Hon. John Cessna, State Sena-

20

tor and member of Congress, was a great grandson of Col. John De Cessna. Another son of the immigrant was Stephen De Cessna, who prior to 1750 was a resident of Cumberland County.

 (1.) See Pa. Mag. of Hist. Vol. III.
 (2.) Will at York, Pa.

COMMENTARIES: COUNT JEAN DE CESSNA

A conflict exists in Howard Cessna's quote of Rev. A. Stapleton's Memorials to the Huguenots as evidence for the history of Jean De Cessna.   Stapleton was researching at the same time as Howard and published his work in 1901.   And Stapleton refers to Howard's research in his footnotes for evidence about the history of our family patriarch.   These two sources are referring to each other as proof for the information they report.

What seems obvious is this: all we know for sure about the first Cessna in America is from the memory of Honorable John Cessna, who served in the US Congress and PA Senate.   He is the most educated and informed voice of the earliest family members who tried to record our tradition.

Stapleton reports two separate spellings for Count Jean: "de Cesna" on page 36 and "de Cessna" on page 129.   Honorable John Cessna reports that this individual stayed in Ireland after the Battle of Boyne. He further reports that he came to Pennsylvania in 1718 with a group of Scotch-Irish who were recruited by William Penn. Elsewhere in his book, Stapleton reports that this migration of "Covenanters" landed at New Castle, Delaware (PA at that time) and then moved north as Penn was able to purchase land from the Indians.

Though he had been granted title to the land by the King, Penn chose to purchase land from the Indians directly to keep peaceful relations.   Pennsylvania was opened to settlement in stages as purchases were made.

About the only thing left to comment on is the name and spelling. "Cessna" is not a French name.   The double "s" is German or Dutch.   However "Cesna" or "Sesna" is a fairly common French name tied directly to the Saxons who settled Normandy.   In French records the name is written with a hard "s" (ß) which is similar in appearance to the German letter that is frequently translated as double "s".

It is reasonable to assume that the Pennsylvania Dutch would write a "ss" for the hard "s" being pronounced by our ancestors.

In House of Cessna Book III, which is currently being written, a long treatise will deal with the names variations in France.   It will also offer a considerable number of historical references of Cesne/Sesne family members dating back to 1060 AD.

John Cessna I

WILL OF JOHN CESSNA 1., PROBATED SEPTEMBER 30, 1751.

Whereas, I, John Cessna, of Newbery, in the County of York, and province of Pensilvenia being very sick and weak in body, but in perfect mind and memmory, praise be given to God, this sixth day of August, in the year of our Lord one thousand seven hundred and fifty-one, Calling to mind ye faility of ye body and desirous to settle my affairs in this world, first of all I recommend my Soul to God that gave it, and my Body to ye Earth to be buried in a Decent Christian manner, and as touching such Worldy goods as it hath pleased God to Bless me with I bestow in ye manner following first that my just Debts and funeral Charges be payd and next I give and bequeath to my true and loving wife Priscilla one fether bed with furniture belonging thereto one Chest of Drawers and all and singular my household goods as also one-third part of the Remainder of my Estate and ye other two-thirds to be divided Equaly between my Children allowing my s'd wife to use ye s'd Childrens parts for her and their supports as Necesesety Requires during her widdowhood, But in case of her second marage to render to ye Children their full shares as before mentioned bearing Intrest from the day of her mariage to be payd to them as soon as they come to age. And I make and ordain my true and loving Wife Priscilla and my trusty and well beloved friend Peter Stout to be my Executrix and Executor of this my last Will and Testament and declare this to be my last Will and Testament as Witness my Hand and Seal ye day and year above written. Signed and Sealed in ye presents of us,

Stephen Foulk
Esther Foulk
Susannah Ward

JOHN CESSNA (Seal.)

COMMENTARY: The Will of John I

Howard Cessna includes the Will of John Cesna (July 1751) in Newberry of York County, PA as being that of the first Cessna in this new world.   He is sometimes referred to as Count Jean De Cessna. Family history records that he was a French Huguenot who fled Normandy in 1685, and fought with William of Orange.   Family tradition says that he is "listed" as a hero in the Cavalry Regiment of Duke de Schomburg.

He would have to have been born in 1665 or sooner.   So he would be at least 85 years old by the time of his death in 1751. Several factors that have been uncovered since Howard Cessna's search indicate that this cannot be the will of an 85 year old man.

His will lists his wife Priscilla Foulke-Cesna and two sons: Stephen and John.   Yet family history also indicates that Count Jean was married in Ireland and had two sons already named Stephen and John.

Records in the Quaker church in Newberry, PA indicate that these two sons and a daughter Ruth were still children.   Priscilla Foulke-Cesna will marry Abraham Elliot in that church a few years after John's death.   Elliot moves the children to North Carolina, and he and Priscilla have at least four more children.

PLEASE NOTE THE FOLLOWING RECORDS:

Quarter Sessions of York County, Pennsylvania; 22 July 1751, "return for a road from Sessney's Fording towards George Croghan's place....begins at

Cesney Fording on Yalow Breeches creek below James Fraziers Mill....north toward Samuel Jones Plantation".

Guilford County, NC: At the Warrington Monthly Meeting (Quaker Church) of July 9, 1763 minutes record the presence Stephen, John and Ruth Sisney from the Newberry Meeting in York County, PA. They are children and are admitted as transfer members in 1765. Other notes from this church state that John Cesna was in attendance at a wedding there in 1749. Minutes also show that Priscilla Foulke-Cesna-Elliott was in the Newberry, PA meeting in July of 1764, and in the Warrington meeting in NC in March of 1765

Foulke Family Records: Record that Priscilla Foulke was married to John Cesna, and that after his death she married Abraham Elliot and moved to Orange County, NC with her children Stephen, John and Ruth.

Cumberland County, PA Orphan's Court: August 1763, Patience Sisney comes asking for guardianship of the inheritance (from her husband Stephen) due her grandchildren: Stephen and John Sisney s/o her son John (deceased); and Stephen Sisney s/o her son Thomas (deceased); during their minority. William Smith is appointed guardian.

Patience Sisney states in court that these two boys (Stephen and John Sisney) are the grandchildren of her and Stephen Sisney and that the John who died in Newberry of York County was their son. Her husband is known to be the son of Count Jean De Cessna and would therefore be the father of the John who married Priscilla Foulke.

It seems unlikely that Count John would have two children named Stephen and John, then late in life marry a younger woman and have two more sons whom he named Stephen and John. And because Priscilla Foulke has more children with Abraham Elliott after their move to North Carolina, it would seem that she was fairly young in

1751. She certainly could not be the wife whom an 85 year old man had met in Ireland some 50 years earlier.

COMENTARY: Stephen Cessna, son of Jean De Cessna

Howard has little to say about the oldest son of our patriarch. Nor, is there speculation about other siblings that came with John and Stephen. The following references tell a discouraging story about this branch of the family. It also offers possibilities of others who came from Ireland also.

Lancaster County Land Records:
Stephen Cessney 200 acres 1 July 1743 bought: 17 Oct 1743
surveyed: 9 Aug 1749 filed
Jacob Sesiney, 100 acres   27 June 1734 surveyed
Christian Sesiney, 150 acres 27 June 1734 surveyed
John Sensiney, 150 acres   25 April 1734 surveyed
Jacob Sensiney, 10 acres   27 Nov 1747 surveyed

Lancaster County Court Records: "the first Tuesday in November 1741" Stephen Sesney is sworn and affirmed on a Grand Inquest

Quarter Sessions minutes for Lancaster County, PA: November 1744, a petition is made for improving a road between Harris' ferry and Stephen Sisney's plantation at the Pine ford on Swatara. Among 29 petitioners are the names Stephen Cessna and John Cessna.

Cumberland County Deed Book: "Stephen Cessna/Sesna, yeoman of Cumberland County and wife Patience make a mortgage to William Dillwood,

Carpenter of Carlisle, on 16 March 1754, 20 pounds for lot 187 in Carlisle, due 1 Oct 1754. Lot was originally own by Thomas Porter".

Book of John Clum, Sheriff of Cumberland County, PA: 6 Oct 1754. Stephen Cessna vs James Long, papers served.

Cumberland County Court Records: April 1756, petition of Stephen Sisney (sick in jail) at the suit of Daniel Hogan, for an unjust debt regarding a hat.

Cumberland County Court Indictments: 5 Oct 1757 comes Arthur Foster and Patience Cessna regarding Administration for Stephen Sisney, "being severly sick, in jail regarding payment for a hat."

Cumberland County Court Records: 18 April 1758, Property of Stephen Sesna, deceased, sheriffed and sold to William Russell of Carlisle, perry-wig maker.

Cumberland County Orphan's Court: August 1763, Patience Sisney comes asking for guardianship of the inheritance (from her husband Stephen) due her grandchildren: Stephen and John Sisney s/o her son John (deceased); and Stephen Sisney s/o her son Thomas (deceased); during their minority. William Smith is appointed guardian.

John Cessna II

THE CAPTURE OF JOHN CESSNA II., BY THE INDIANS

(Pa. Archives vol. iii. p. 219.)

A list of those killed and missing at John Cisney's field, about seven miles from Shippensburg, on July 18th, 1757. Killed: John Kirkpatrick, Dennie O'Neidon. Missing: John Cisney and three small boys, two sons of Cisney, and one a son of John Kirkpatrick.

The History of Cumberland County, Pa., page 251, under head of Indian Murders. contains the following: On July 18, 1757, a band of savages surprised a party who were harvesting in a field belonging to John Cessna, about a mile east of Shippensburg. The Indians approached the field from the east through the woods which bounded it on that side and when within a short range fired, killing Kirkpatrick and O'Neidon; then rushing forward they captured Mr. Cessna, his two grandsons and a son of Kirkpatrick and made their escape with their prisoners.

In the same book, page 260, we learn that settlements were made at a very early day southeast of Shippensburg. John Dunlap, John Cessna, et al., owned large tracts of land. East of the tract of land now owned by Ira L. Long is where John Cessna was captured. The land remained in possession of the descendants of John Cessna until 1827.

HOW THE INDIANS TREATED PRISONERS

Narrative of Marie Le Roy and Barbara Leininger.

These two girls were captured by the Indians in middle Pennsylvania about the time John Cessna (II.) was captured near Shippensburg, Pa. Only a portion of the statement given to the public by them as found in Vol. ii., Penn'a. Archives, page 403, etc., is here produced, enough being given to show the disposition of the Indians at that time towards their prisoners:

"Early in the morning of Oct. 16th, 1775, while Le Roy's hired man went out to fetch the cows, he heard the Indians shooting six times, soon after eight of them came to the house and killed Marie Le Roy's father with tomahawks. Her brother defending himself desperately, for a time, but was at last overpowered. The Indians did not kill him, but took him prisoner, together with Marie Le Roy and a little girl who was staying with the family. Thereupon they plundered the homestead, and set it on fire. Into this fire they laid the body of the murdered father, feet foremost, until it was half consumed. The upper half was left lying on the ground, with the two tomahawks, with which they had killed him, sticking in his head. Then they kindled another fire not far from the house. While sitting around it, a neighbor of Le Roy, named Bastian, happened to pass by on horseback. He was immediately shot down and scalped.

Two of the Indians now went to the house of Barbara Leininger, where they found her father, her brother, and her sister, Regina. Her mother had gone to the mill. They demanded rum, but there was none in the house. Then they called for tobacco, which was given them. Having filled and smoked a pipe, they said: "We are Alleghany Indians, and your enemies. You must all die." Thereupon they shot her father, tomahawked her brother, who was twenty years of age, took Barbara and her sister, Regina, prisoners, and conveyed them into the forest for about a mile. There they were soon joined by the other Indians, with Marie Le Roy and the little girl. Not long after several of the Indians led the prisoners to the top of a high hill near the two plantations. Towards evening the rest of the savages returned with six fresh and bloody scalps, which they threw at the feet of the poor captives, saying that they had a good hunt that day.

The next morning we were taken about two miles further into the forest, while the most of the Indians again went out to kill and plunder. Towards evening they returned with nine scalps and five prisoners.

On the third day the whole band came together and divided the spoils. In addition to large quantities of provisions, they had taken 14 horses, 10 prisoners, namely: One man, one woman, five girls, and three boys. We two girls, as also two of the horses, fell to the share of an Indian named Galasko.

We traveled with our new master for two days. He was tolerably kind, and allowed us to ride all the way, while he and the rest of the Indians walked. Of this circumstance Barbara Leininger took advantage, and tried to escape. But she was almost immediately recaptured, and condemned to be burned alive. The savages gave her a French Bible, which they had taken from Le Roy's house, in order that she might prepare for death; and, when she told them that she could not understand it, they gave her a German Bible. Thereupon they made a larger pile of wood and set it on fire, intending to put her into the midst of it. But a young Indian begged so earnestly for her life that she was pardoned, after having promised not to attempt to escape again, and to stop her crying." (Here follows a description of route traveled being through what is now Clearfield and Jefferson Counties, Pa., stopping at Kittanny.) "As this was to be the place of our permanent abode, we here received our welcome, according to Indian custom. It consisted of three blows each, on the back. They were, however, administered with great mercy. Indeed, we concluded that we were beaten merely in order to keep up an ancient usage, and not with the intention of injuring us. * * * * * * The Indians gave us enough to do. We had to tan leather, to make shoes (moccasins), to clear land, to plant corn, to cut down trees and build huts, to wash and cook. The want of provisions, however, caused us the greatest sufferings. During all the time that we were at Kittanny, (almost a year), we had neither lard nor salt; and, sometimes, we were forced to live on acorns, roots, grass, and bark. There was nothing in the world to make this new sort of food palatable, excepting hunger itself. * * * * * * There we had the mournful opportunity of witnessing the cruel end of an English woman, who had attempted to flee out of her captivity and to return to the settlements of Col. Armstrong. Having been recaptured by the savages, and brought back to Kittanny, she was put to death in an unheard of way. First, they scalped her; next, they laid burning splinters of wood, here and there, upon her body; and then they cut off her ears and fingers, forcing them into her mouth so that she had to swallow them. Amidst such torments, this woman lived from nine o'clock in the morning until towards sunset, when a French officer took compassion on her, and put her out of her misery. An English soldier, on the contrary, named John ———, who escaped from prison at Lancaster, and joined the French, had a piece of flesh cut from her body and ate it. When she was dead, the Indians chopped her in two, through the middle, and let her lie until the dogs came and devoured her. Three days later an Englishman was brought in, who had likewise attempted to escape with Col Armstrong, and burned alive in the same village. His torments, however, continued only about three hours; but his screams were frightful to listen to. It rained that day very hard, so that the Indians could not keep up the fire. Hence they began to discharge gunpowder at his body. At last, amidst his worst pains, when the poor man called for a drink of water, they brought him melted lead, and poured it down his throat. This draught at once helped him out of the hands of the barbarians for he died on the instant.

. It is easy to imagine what an impression such fearful instances of cruelty make upon the mind of a poor captive. Does he attempt to escape from the savages, he knows in advance that, if taken, he will be roasted alive. * * * * * * After having, in the past three years seen no one of our own flesh and blood, except those unhappy beings who, like ourselves, were bearing the yoke of the heaviest slavery, we had the unexpected pleasure of meeting with a German, who was not a captive but free and who, as we heard, had been sent into this neighborhood to negotiate peace between the English and natives. His name was Frederick Post. We, and all the other prisoners, heartily wished him success and God's blessing upon his undertaking. We were, however, not allowed to speak with him. The Indians gave us plainly to understand that any attempt to do this would be taken amiss. He himself, by the reserve with which he treated us, let us see that this was not the time to talk over our afflictions. But we were greatly alarmed on his account.

(Here follows plan for escape, including two young Englishmen and the two girls.)

"We had to pass many huts inhabited by the savages, and knew that there were at least sixteen dogs with them. In the merciful providence of God not a single one of these dogs barked. Their barking would at once have betrayed us, and frustrated our design. It is hard to describe the anxious fears of a poor woman under such circumstances. The extreme probability that the Indians would pursue, and recapture us, was as two to one compared with the dim hope that, perhaps, we would get through in safety. But even if we escaped the Indians, how would we ever succeed in passing through the wilderness, unacquainted with a single path or trail, without a guide, and helpless, half naked, broken down by more than three years of hard slavery, hungry and scarcely any food, the season wet and cold, and many rivers and streams to cross? If one could not believe that there is a God, who helps and saves from death, one had better let

33

running away alone.

We safely reached the river—Muskingum, (southern part of Ohio). Here the first thought in all our minds was: O! that we were safely across! And Barbara Leininger, in particular, recalling prayers from an old hymn, which she had learned in her youth, put them together, to suit our present circumstances something in the following style:

> O bring us safely across this river!
> In fear I cry, yea my soul doth quiver.
> The worst afflictions are now before me,
> Wher:'er I turn nought but death do I see.

(The above is about one-fifth of the prayer as given.)

Presently we found a raft, left by the Indians. Thanking God that He had himself prepared a way for us across these first waters we got on board and pushed off. But we were carried almost a mile down the river before we could reach the other side. There our journey began in good earnest. Full of anxiety and fear, we fairly ran that whole night and all next day, when we lay down to rest without venturing to kindle a fire. Early the next morning, Owen Gibson fired at a bear. The animal fell, but, when he ran with his tomahawk to kill it, it jumped up and bit him in the feet, leaving three wounds. We all hastened to his assistance. The bear escaped into narrow holes among the rocks, where we could not follow. On the third day, however, Owen Gibson shot a deer. We cut off the hind-quarters and roasted them at night. The next morning he again shot a deer, which furnished us with food for that day. In the evening we got to the Ohio river, having made a circuit of over one hundred miles in order to reach it." * * * *

After telling how they crossed the Ohio; provisions being all; about both Barbara and Marie falling into the water and almost drowning; Owen Gibson losing his flint and steel, causing them to spend four nights without fire amidst rain and snow; about the soldiers at Fort Pittsburg, being reluctant to extend help at first thinking they were Indians— they tell of their journey east through Pennsylvania, stopping here at Fort Bedford one week (Gibson remained at Bedford) and arriving at Philadelphia Sunday, May 6th.

Military Record of Cessnas Serving in Revolutionary War.

CAPT. CHARLES CESSNA

(Vol. ix., Pa. Archives, p. 236.)

BEDFORD, June 30, 1781.

To Col. James Morgan.

Sir:—The bearer, Mr. Isaac Warrell, one of my Deputies in the purchasing way in this county—goes to you for the express purpose of getting your advice in order to direct and govern in the Departments. The distress of this county is truly great, murders and depredations are committed almost every week and not a single article can be had for the money that's now current. I am even threatened and inveighed against by the people for not having suitable provisions for such as do military duty, and it is impossible for me to get it for the money I have; I am indebted to numbers in consequence of such articles as we purchased and so are my Deputies, having engaged on the credit of the money and which is now useless; and unless something be done in order to enable us to get provisions for such as are employed in protecting the county, I am afraid the settlement may break up totally and that very soon. It is impossible for me to send you an accurate return having purchased on the credit of the money which was in so fluctuating a state while it dubiously passed as to leave no room for a certain price in any article; and now no person would receive any quantity of it for a single beef cattle, I beg you will dispatch the Bearer with all due haste and I hope in such a manner equipped as will enable me and those that are employed by me in the service to do the requisite and necessary Duty expected of us. I am sir, with great respect,

Your most obed't H'ble sev't,

CHAS. CESSNA.

(Vol ix. Pa. Archives, p. 467.)

December 17, 1781.

To Honorable General Potter,

Sir:—Considering the agreement made by us, and entered on the Council Books, a Doubt has suggested on account of carriage.

The only place in our county fit for storing Provisions in, is the town of Bedford, which is, in every Direction, a considerable Distance from such places as are capable of making the necessary Defence.

It is 55 miles distant from Lead Mine Gap, 40 from the Gap of Frankston, and also 40 from Conemaugh. These are the common passes through which the enemy penetrates into the country.

And sending Provisions to all or any of these posts, will be attended with expences, and which might be entirely out of our power to defray.

To neglect giving this necessary information to Council, would be in some measure criminal in us; forasmuch as the want of such knowledge might lead into great mistake, by which expectations wou'd take place, and, of course, disappointments ensue very interesting to the distressed Frontiers; for unless punctuality is observed, it will frustrate and render useless the salutary Measures adopted by Government for the Defence of the Frontiers. We therefore pray the sense of his excellency and the Honorable Board of Council on this subject.

We are, sir your obed't, H'ble, Servts,

BERNARD DOUGHERTY,

CHARLES CESSNA.

(Vol. 13 Col. Rec. p. 298.)

PHILADELPHIA, June 5, 1782.

The following order was drawn on the Treasury, viz:
In favor of Charles Cessna, Esq., for the sum of 100
pounds—state money of 7th of Apr., 1781—being extra
allowance for his service as commissioner of Purchase in
the county of Bedford. Also in favor of said Charles Cessna
for the sum of 100 pounds sp. ie, to be by him delivered to
Mess. Cessna and Dougherty—contractors for supplying
with provisions the Ranging Company and militia in actual
service in the county of Bedford.

(Vol 13, Col. Rec. p. 133-134.)

Nov. 30, 1781.

An order was drawn on Treasurer for Charles Cessna
and Bernard Dougherty. Also returns of election for Bedford county made known which shows that Charles Cessna
was elected Representative, and John Cessna Sheriff. The
sureties of John Cessna were Charles Cessna and Allen
Ross.

(Vol. 11 Col. Rec. p. 363.)

LANCASTER, Oct. 30, 1777.

The returns of the general election for Bedford county
show Charles Cessna to have been elected one of the Representatives; also Jno. Cessna to be elected Sheriff.

(Bedford County History, p. 76.)

Shows Chas. Cessna to have been one of the first grand
jurors of Bedford county.

(Same History, p. 69.)

Assessors returns of 1772 show in Cumberland Valley:
John Cessna, 250 acres; improved, 12.

Charles Cessna, 290 acres; improves, 20; 1 servant, 2
horses, 2 cows.

Evan Cessna, 200 acres; improved, 12.

Vol. 14 Pa. Arch. (2nd series) p. 656·shows Charles
Cessna to have been Major of the 2nd Battalion July, 1776.
Maj. John Cessna marched with this Battalion as a volun-

teer. In same book Charles Cessna appears as Colonel of 1st Battalion,. p. 658-671.

(Vol. 12 Colonial Records, p. 303.)

PHIL'A., Apr. 3, 1780.

In Council—Resolved that the Quarter Master General of the Army be informed that this Board have appointed the following persons commissioners of purchasers, agreeable to the late Act of Assembly. Charles Cessna, Esq., for the county of Bedford. (Here follows the names of eleven others appointed throughout the State). They were each required to give security in 500 pounds each for the due performance of their office.

In the Auditor General's Department at Harrisburg, Pa., I saw the returns of purchases made by Charles Cessna, same being in his hand writing which is very legible written.

In vol. 12 Col. Rec., p. 371, appears an order in favor of Chas. Cessna, Esq., for the sum of 500 pounds of money, same to be used in purchasing in Bedford county.

WILLIAM CESSNA III.

Pa. Arch. vol. 14 (2nd series) p. 410, shows William Cessna to have been 2nd Lieutenant of 5th Company in 6th Battalion July 31, 1777. In same book, p. 435, he appears also as 2nd Lieutenant of 5th Company, 6th Battalion, May 14, 1778.

EVAN CESSNA III.

Bedford County History, p. 69, shows Evan Cessna to have been assessed for 200 acres with 12 acres improved, being in Cumberland Valley township in 1772.

Pa. Arch. Vol. 14 (2nd series) p. 672, shows Evan Cessna to be Captain of 3rd Company, 1st Battalion of Pennsylvania soldiers, 1781. In same book, p. 680, Evan Cessna was Captain of undesignated militia, 1782.

Following is a list of some of the Cessnas serving in the different wars of the past:

SPANISH WAR

Sergeant J. S. Cessna, Co. 7, U. S. V. Signal Corps. See article published in Bedford Gazette, Oct. 7, 1898.

Otis Jay Cessna, Battle Creek, Mich.

Ed Walters, son of Mrs. Kate (Cisne) Walters, of Fairfield, Ill., 9th Reg. Band, Ill. See article published in Fairfield Sun, Feb. 11, 1899.

CIVIL WAR

Col. William Cessna, Kenton, O.

Dr. B. F. Cessna, Kenton, O.

Dr. J. P. Cessna, Canfield, O.

Five brothers, sons of James, V., (William IV.), served under Gen. Phil. Sheridan, 2nd U. S. C.

Wm. Cessna, V., (Sq. James IV.) Bedford, Pa.

MEXICAN WAR

W. F. Cessna, Friend's Cove, Bedford county, Pa.

WAR OF 1812

Stephen Cessna (IV.), Stephen (III.). Served with Capt. Brush, of Chillocothe, O.

Wm. Cessna, a great-grand uncle of James Martin, of Philadelphia, Pa., who has control of all Pullman cars used east of Chicago, Ill., was with General Harrison and passed through the campaign at Erie. He died at the house of Mrs. McCauslin, at Bedford, in 1862, when the Bucktail Regiment was in camp close to Bedford and was buried with the honors of war.

REVOLUTIONARY WAR

Maj. John Cessna, Vol. XI. Colonial Records, p. 123.

Maj. John Cessna, Vol. XII. Colonial Records, p. 575.

Maj. John Cessna, Vol. 14 or 13, 2nd series Pa. Archives, pages 642-643.

Maj. John Cessna, Vol. XIV., 2nd series Pa. Archives, page 644.

Maj. John Cessna, Vol II., 2nd series Pa. Archives, page 511.

Col Charles Cessna, Vol. IX., Pa. Archives, pages 36 and 467.

Col. Charles Cessna, Vol. XIV., 2nd series Pa. Archives, pages 642 and 644.

P 105 Capt. Evan Cessna, Vol. XIV., 2nd series Pa. Archives, pages 658-667.

P. 105 Jonathan Cessna, Vol. XIV., 2nd series Pa. Archives, page 667.

100 Stephen Cessna, Vol. XIV., 2nd series Pa. Archives, page 18.

William Cessna, Vol. XIV., 2nd series Pa. Archives, 6th Battalion, 5th Co., pages 410-435.

FRENCH AND INDIAN WAR

See "Coal of Arms" pamphlet
p.12-14 for later information

John Cessna III.

Charles Cessna III.

JOHN CESSNA (III.), John (II.), John (I.)

Born Jan. 26, 1726, died March 31, 1802. Married (1) Sarah Rose, who was born Feb. 6, 1740, died July 1, 1788. Issue: Jonathan (Nov. 16, 1760) 1, Rachel (Aug. 1,1762) 2, John (Dec. 8, 1764) 3. *P. 37*

P. 25 The date of this birth differs with date given in book of Rebecca Smith's. This date is taken from book of J. Wilson Cessna, of Nevada, Iowa, and owing to the correctness of other dates, I infer this to be the proper

see p. 44 - deaths

See p. 43-44

See p. 100   p. 44-45

record. Stephen (Dec. 28, 1766) 4, Elizabeth (Dec. 1, 1768) 5, William (June 20, 1775) 6.

p. 98   p. 99

Married (2) Elizabeth Hall. Issue: Evan 1, Charles 2, James 3, and a daughter who died at the age of 20.

On one of the pages in the Bible kept by John Cessna (III.) is written the following:

ON BACK OF BOOK.

Where will the wrath for shelter fly
That does thy God of love defy,
And will not to his call attend
Although he is their only friend.

They may awhile his power defy
And call for vengeance from the sky,
The Lord will vengeance on them pore
In storms of wrath to cease no more.

REVOLUTIONARY WAR RECORD OF MAJOR JOHN CESSNA

(Vol. 11, Col. Rec., p. 123.)

PHILADELPHIA, Feb. 13, 1777.

Capt. Bickham was directed to pay Maj. Coomb £75, 10, 6, for subsistance of himself, Maj. Cisna, a Capt. and 23 men of Col. Wood's Battalion, Bedford county.

(Vol. 12, Col. Rec., p. 19.)

June 10, 1779.

A return of Justices elect, chosen for the Township of Colerain, in Bedford county, shows that Abraham Milley and John Cisney were elected.

(Vol. 12, Col. Rec., p. 147.)

PHILADELPHIA, Oct. 25, 1779.

Returns of General Election show John Cesna to have been elected Sheriff.

(Vol. 12, Col. Rec., p. 575.)

PHILA., Dec. 19, 1780.

In Council.—Col. Piper, member of this Board, Bedford county, having represented that Maj. John Cessna, in consequence of orders from a committee, dated July 14, 1776, signed by Mess. Woods, Smith, Galbreath, Espy, Dougherty, Nagel and Davidson, and also upon a like

41

direction from Col. Woods, dated Jan. 6, 1777, had taken the arms of persons who did not go themselves into service; and that for the execution of said orders, he is now prosecuted at common law.

Resolved, That all officers not abusing their powers, ought to be indemnified by the public; that therefore this Board direct the Atty. General, or his Deputy to defend said suit at the charge of this Commonwealth, if on inquiry he shall find that Maj. Cessna is prosecuted for the performance of such public service, and has not acted oppressively therein; and that in case of the absence of the Atty. General, or his Deputy, the Court of Common Pleas appoint some gentlemen of the law to defend said suit at the public expense.

(Maj. John Cessna was vindicated and all his expense paid by the State of Pennsylvania.)

(Bedford County History, p. 86.)

Maj. John Cessna marched as a volunteer with a Bedford county company arriving in camp Jan. 9, 1777.

In Pa. Arch. Vol. 14, (2nd series), p. 657, he appears as the Field officer. On page 659 in same book he is shown to have been one of the officers Dec. 10, 1777, to form the Board of Court Martial.

COLERAIN TOWNSHIP, BEDFORD CO., PA.

A description of Colerain township, taken from Bedford County History, where Maj. John Cessna (III.) first settled in Bedford county, having purchased the farm from the first U. S. Senator of Pennsylvania—Wm. McClay.

(Bedford County History, p. 353.

Colerain was organized as a township of Cumberland County, prior to the formation of Bedford County in 1771. Its original dimensions cannot be ascertained, though there is evidence that it covered nearly one-third of the present territory of the county.

The nearness of Friend's Cove to Fort Bedford was favorable to early settlement, and the white man came early to this beautiful valley. During the trying scenes that ensued, the pioneers bore themselves with firmness and courage. The Revolutionary period presented the darkest scenes in the early history of Bedford County, and the inhabitants of Friend's Cove were subjected, during that time, to the greatest dangers and hardships. The reader is referred to the general history for an account of the contests between the white men and the Indians. It is the purpose of the present chapter to deal with the people and their achievement in this particular locality.

Friend's Cove is a fertile and beautiful valley, encompassed by mountains on three sides. The soil is of more than usual fertility, and the land, though somewhat stony, is valuable to agriculturists. The first pioneers generally located at or very near the foot of the mountains, on what would not be considered the least valuable portion of the valley. The reason for this was, doubtless, the fear of frosts, which were very prevalent along the bottom lands and in all low places.

John Friend, for whom the Cove is named, secured a title to a tract of land lying at the southern end of the borough of Rainsburg, which was patented to him as "Friend's Retreat," in 1762. A portion of the Friend's farm is now owned by George W. Williams, and a part is included within the borough. Joseph Friend, another pioneer, lived upon an ajacent tract.

Whence the Friend's came, or how they lived and what perils they encountered, cannot now be ascertained. The only record they have left of themselves is in the name which the valley bears. Doubtless they were adventurous hunters, and subsisted on game, paying slight attention to the tilling of the soil.

Almost contemporary with the Friends came the Cessna family, from the eastern portion of the State, who settled, in 1765, on land which is still in the Cessna name.

The Cessnas are of Huguenot ancestry and are descended from John Cessna, who came from southern France to America in 1690, after the Battle of the Boyne, in which he participated. John Cessna, who settled in Friend's Cove in 1765, was his grand-son. The latter was prominent in the affairs of the county at the beginning of its existence and served three terms as Sheriff. He was also a member of the constitutional convention of 1774, which drafted the first constitution of the State of Pennsylvania. He was the father of 13 children by his first wife. At the age of 70 he married a second wife, and of this union five children were born. He died in 1802, at the age of 76. His son, John, succeeded to the ownership of the farm. John the second died in 1813. Of his sons only William and Samuel lived to mature years. His daughters were: Sarah (James), Rachel (Jackson), Ellen (McGashlin), and Elizabeth (Morgart). William Cessna, the father of Hon. John Cessna, of Bedford, was born in 1799, and died in 1864. He married Rachel Morgart, and their children were: John, Peter Morgart (deceased), Rebecca (Smith), Mary (Bowles), Thomas R, Rachel (Smith), Joseph, Christina A. (Cunningham), William, George W., Jonathan B., and Martha (deceased). William Cessna became the owner of the Cessna homestead in 1819; his son, William, now owns it and resides upon it.

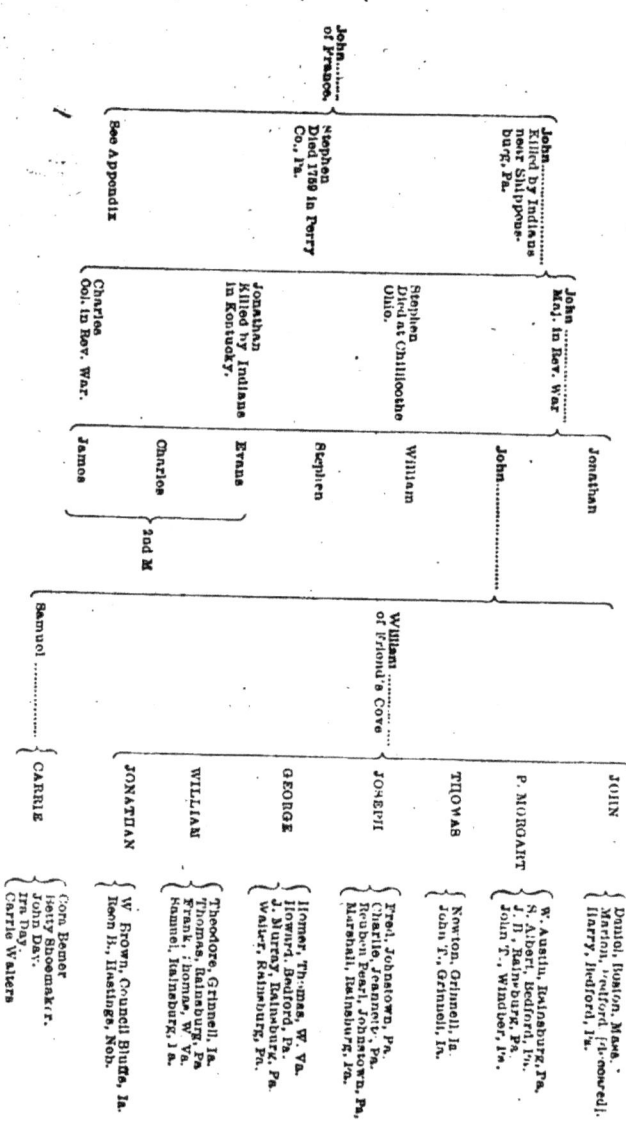

44

John Cessna IV, John III,
John II, John I.

Born October 16, 1768, died August 5, 1813. Lived on the Cessna farm, one mile west of Rainsburg, Pa. Married Mary McCauslin March 2, 1786. She died July 25, 1825. Issue: (1) John, born February, 1787, died April, 1787, (2) Sally, born May 6, 1788. (3) Margaret, born September 6, 1789, died September 25, 1806. (4) Mary, born August 2, 1791, died September 23, 1806. (5) John, born April 1793, died February 1796. (6) Elizabeth, born January 17, 1795. (7) Rachel, born February 7, 1797. (8). William, born January 11, 1799. (9). Samuel, born October 15, 1800. (10) John, born July 4, 1802, died September 29, 1806. (11) Margaret, born March 6, 1805. (12) Eleanor, born May 20, 1807. See p 43 for (12) marriage.

SALLY CESSNA V, JOHN IV.

Married George James. Occupation, farmer in Friend's Cove. Issue: (1) John, (2) William, (3) Ellen, (4) Alexander, (5) Samuel, (6) Sarah, (7) Rachel, (8) George, (9) Maggie.

2. marriages. RACHEL CESSNA V, JOHN IV.

Born 1796. Married (1) E. Rogers, of Bedford, Pa. Issue: Alexander. Married (2) a Mr. Jackson, a farmer of Council Bluffs, Iowa. Issue: (1) Andrew, (2) Mary (Dunken), (3) Ellen (Record), (4) Franklin, (5) James, (6) Margaret, (7) John, (8) Wilson.

46

ELIZABETH CESSNA V, JOHN IV

Married Peter Morgart. Issue: (1) John, (2) Baltz, (3) Perry, (4) Frank, (5) Samuel, (6) Benjamin, (7) Ellen (Hafer), (8) Mary (Buchanan), (9) Rebecca (Evans), (10) Rachel (Perrin), (11) Eliza (Fitzsimmons).

ELLEN CESSNA V, JOHN IV

Married (1) Rev. Gasten. Issue: Three children. Married (2) Thomas C. McGavern. Address, Denver, Colo., later Helena, or Butte, Montana.

SAMUEL CESSNA V, JOHN IV

Married Margaret Moss. Issue: Carrie Cessna.

CARRIE CESSNA VI, Samuel v

Married (1) Mr. Crampton. Issue: (1) Cora, who married Mr. Beemer, (2) Betty, who married Mr. Shoemocker. Issue: (1) Edith, (2) Cora, (3) Ida. Address, Baltimore, Md.

Married (2) Ira Day. Issue. (1) John, (2) Ira, (3) Carrie. Carrie married William Walters. Issue: (1) George, (2) Susan, (3) Margaret. Address, Baltimore, Md.

WILLIAM CESSNA V, JOHN IV

Born January 11, 1799, died 1864. Married Rachel Morgart who died November 21, 1860, aged 62 years and 21 days. Issue: (1) John, (2) P. Morgart, (3) Rebecca, (4) Mary, (5) Thomas, (6) Rachel, (7) Joseph, (8) Christiana (Tena), (9) George W., (10) William, (11) Jonathan B.

Oct. 31, 1798

WILLIAM CESSNA VI, William v, John iv.

Address, Rainsburg, Pa. Occupation, retired farmer. Married Rachel Rose, of Greenwood, Indiana, in 1862. Issue: (1) Lillie, (2) Cora, (3) Theodore, (4) Thomas, (5) Frank, (6) Samuel, (7) Ella.

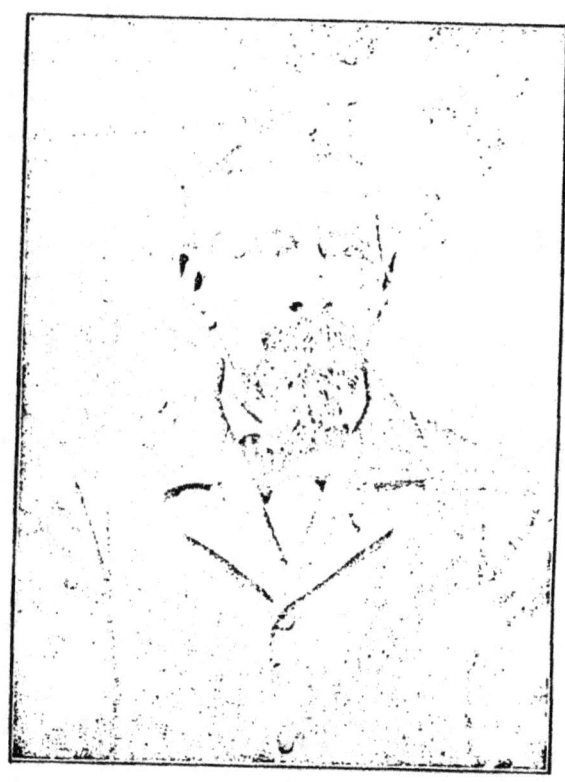

WILLIAM CESSNA.
Page 26.

JOSEPH CESSNA.
Page 27.

49

LILLIE CESSNA, (VII), William, (VI).

Address, Rainsburg, Pa. Single.

CORA CESSNA, (VII), William, (VI).

Address, Rainsburg, Pa. Single.

THEODORE CESSNA, (VII), William, (VI).

Address, Grinnell, Iowa. Occupation, farmer and stockman. Married Ella Bucannon. Issue:

THOMAS CESSNA, (VII), William, (VI).

Address, Rainsburg, Pa. Occupation, huckster. Married Jane Howser. Issue:

FRANK CESSNA, (VII), William, (VI).

Address, Rainsburg, Pa. Occupation, dairyman. Married Laura Perdew. Issue: (1) Alma Elizabeth, born August 3, 1897, (2) William Curtin, born May 13, 1899.

SAMUEL CESSNA, (VII), William, (VI).

Address, Rainsburg, Pa. Occupation, farmer. Married Etta Diehl. No issue.

ELLA CESSNA, (VII), William, (VI).

Address, Rainsburg, Pa. Married Marion Filler, a carpenter. Issue: (1) Rose.

JOSPH CESSNA VI, William v, John iv

Address, Rainsburg, Pa. Occupation, stock dealer. Born May 9, 1832. Married Elizabeth Filler. Issue: (1) Martha (died young), (2) Anna Belle, (3) Rebecca, (4) Johnny (died young), (5) Fred, (6) Alice (died young), (7)

Charles Edward, (8) Ella, (9) Reuben, (10) Pearl, (11) Hattie, (12) Marshal.

ANNA BELLE CESSNA, (VII), Joseph, (VI).

Address, Bedford, Pa. Born January 9, 1861. Married Alonzo F. Smith, a salesman. Issue: Gladys, aged 16, Rheon, Fred, Charlie.

REBECCA CESSNA, (VII), Joseph, (VI).

Address, Frostburg, Md. Born March 14, 1863. Married John Gump, a saddler. Issue: (1) Grace, age 15, (2) Orval, (3) Elizabeth, (4) Charlie.

FRED CESSNA, (VII), Joseph, (VI).

Address, Johnstown, Pa Born February 25, 1867. Occupation, collector. Married Annie Woodhead. Issue: Joseph Marshall.

CHARLES E. CESSNA, (VII), Joseph, (VI).

Address, Johnstown, Pa. Born March 12, 1871. Occupation, salesman. Married Ada Shaffer. Issue:

ELLA CESSNA, (VII), Joseph, (VI).

Born October 3, 1873. Single.

REUBEN CESSNA, (VII), Joseph (VI).

Born September 16, 1875. Single.

HATTIE CESSNA, (VII), Joseph, (VI).

Born November 3, 1877. Single.

MARSHALL CESSNA, (VII), Joseph, (VI).

Born January 21, 1880. Single.

P. MORGART CESSNA VI, William v, John iv.

Born September 12, 1822, died July 6, 1861, aged 38 years, 9 months and 21 days. Occupation, farmer. Married Margaret Stuckey. Issue: (1) William Austin, (2) Simon Albert, (3) John T., (4) J. Buchanan, (5) Jennie, (6) Adda.

WILLIAM AUSTIN CESSNA, (VII), P. Morgart, (VI).

Age 50. Address, Rainsburg, Pa. Occupation, stockman. Married Lottie Filler. Issue: (1) Fannie, (2) Gertrude, (3) Nellie, (4) Ralph, (5) Reta, (6) Chester, (7) Raymond, (8) Charles Paul, (9) Pearl Daisy, (10) Ruth.

FANNIE CESSNA, (VIII), William Austin, (VII).

Address, Johnstown, Pa. Occupation, Nurse.

GERTRUDE CESSNA, (VIII), William Austin, (VII).

Address, Centreville, Pa. Married Walter Hite. Issue: (1) Charlotte Louisa.

All the other children of William Austin, (VII), as above named are single and live at home.

SIMON ALBERT CESSNA, (VII), P. Morgart, (VI).

Address, Bedford, Pa. Age, about 51. Born April 7, 1852. Business, former County Treasurer of Bedford County, Pa. Married Anna R. James. Issue: (1) H. Bertram, attorney-at-law at the bar of Bedford County, (2) Maude, (3) Grace, (4) Clyde. All single.

JOHN T. CESSNA, (VII), P. Morgart, (VI).

Address, Rainsburg, Pa. Occupation, salesman. Married (1) Annie James. Issue: Flora, age 16. Married (2) Miss Shaffer. Issue: (1) Margaret, (2) Lamont.

J. BUCHANAN CESSNA, (VII), P. Morgart, (VI).

Address, Rainsburg, Pa. Married Miss Etta Gump.

ADDA CESSNA, (VII), P. Morgart, (VI).

Address, Rainsburg, Pa. Married Fred Hardsauc, a silver-smith. Issue: Linnie.

JENNIE CESSNA, (VII), P. Morgart, (VI).

Address, Rainsburg, Pa. Single.

GEORGE W. CESSNA VI, William v, John iv.

Born March 30, 1838. Address, Rainsburg, Pa. Occupation, tanner. Married Emma McElfish. Issue: (1) Ida, (2) Homer, (3) Della, (4) Howard, (5) George Leighton, born May 13, 1873, died March 24, 1874. (6) Bertha, (7) Murray, (8) Walter, (9) Rachel, born February 3, 1883, died March 11, 1883. (10) Anna.

(John W. McElfish b. Dec. 12, 1808. Married Rachel Middleton, b. Dec. 6, 1814.)

IDA CESSNA, (VII), George, (VI).

Born January 10, 1865. Address, Bedford, Pa. Married Prof. D. C. Stunkard Principal of Bedford Public Schools. Issue: (1) Marguerite, (2) Lamonte.

HOMER CESSNA, (VII), George, (VI).

Born November 1, 1866. Address, Rainsburg, Pa. Occupation, tanner. Married Annie Campbell. Issue: Edith.

DELLA CESSNA, (VII), George, (VI).

Born December 7, 1868. Address, 521 North Charles Street, Baltimore, Md. Married Dr. A. C. Brewer. Issue: Mary.

GEORGE W. CESSNA.
Page 30.

HOWARD CESSNA, (VII), George, (VI).

Born October 27, 1870. Address, Bedford, Pa. Single. Occupation, attorney-at-law.

BERTHA CESSNA, (VII), George, (VI).

Born December 18, 1874. Address, Rainsburg, Pa. Single.

MURRAY CESSNA, (VII), George, (VI).

Born July 28, 1877. Address, Rainsburg, Pa. Dental surgeon. Single.

WALTER CESSNA, (VII), George, (VI).

Born December 21, 1880. Address, Rainsburg, Pa. Single.

ANNA CESSNA, (VII), George, (VI).

Born June 25, 1887. Single. Student at Juniata College, Huntingdon, Pa.

HON. JOHN CESSNA VI, William v, John iv.

Born June 29, 1821. Married Ellen Shaffer. Issue: (1) Dan, (2) Carrie, (3) Marion, (4) Etta, (5) Harry. Was Congressman and held many positions of trust—See Biography. Died December 13. 1893.

DAN CESSNA, (VII), John, (VI).

Address, Bedford, Pa. Occupation, salesman. Married Ella Reamer, of Kentucky. No issue.

CARRIE CESSNA, (VII), John, (VI).

Married Rev. Layton Gerhart, of Lancaster, Pa. Issue: (1) Paul Cessna, (2) Florence, (3) Edith, (4) Arthur.

MARION CESSNA, (VII), John, (VI).

Died 1893, aged about 40. Occupation, electrician. Married Jennie Elliot. Issue: John.

ETTA CESSNA, (VII), John, (VI).

Address, Bedford, Pa. Married Hon. E. S. Doty, a member of the Legislature and Cashier of First National Bank of Bedford, Pa. Issue: (1) James Cloyd, (2) Ellen Cessna.

HARRY CESSNA, (VII), John, (VI).

Address, Bedford, Pa. Occupation, attorney-at-law. Married Flora Eaby, of Lancaster, Pa. Issue: (1) George, (2) Helen.

MARY CESSNA VI, William v, John iv.

Address, Bedford, Pa. Born, December 16, 1825. Married Jeremiah K. Bowles, a merchant and at one time postmaster of Bedford, Pa. Issue: (1) Martha Alice, (2) William Cessna, (3) Mary Bell, (4) Annie Rebecca, (5) John Sample (died young), (6) Rachel Ellen.

MARTHA ALICE BOWLES, (VII), Mary, (VI), William, (V).

Address, Bedford, Pa. Married John McClintock. No issue. Was postmistress of Bedford, Pa.

WILLIAM CESSNA BOWLES, (VII), Mary, (VI), William, (V).

Address, Elizabeth, N. J. Occupation, civil engineer. Married Caroline Scout. Issue: William Henry.

THOMAS R. CESSNA.
Page 33.

MARY BELLE BOWLES, (VII), Mary, (VI), William, (V).

Address, Cumberland, Md. Married Joseph W. Galbreath, a civil engineer. Issue: Mary Bowles.

ANNIE REBECCA BOWLES, (VII), Mary, (VI), William, (V).

Address, Bedford, Pa. Married D. W. Prosser. No issue.

RACHEL ELLEN BOWLES, (VII), Mary, (VI), William, (V).

Address, Everett, Pa. Married Benjamin F. Ashcom, a merchant. No issue.

THOMAS R. CESSNA VI, William v, John iv.

Occupation, retired farmer. Address, Grinnell, Iowa. Born Ortober 27, 1827. Married Sarah Koerner. Issue: (1) Laura, (2) Ella, (3) Newton, (4) Belle, (5) John T., (6) Hattie, (7) Myrtle.

LAURA CESSNA, (VII), Thomas R., (VI).

Address, Grinnell, Iowa. Born July 18, 1849. Married Samuel Burnside, of Blue Grass, Iowa. Occupation, farmer. (1) Nettie (dead), (2) Leroy (dead), (3-4) Clinton and Clifton (twins), (5) Lulu.

ELLA CESSNA, (VII), Thomas R., (VI).

Address, Grinnell, Iowa. Born November 4, 1853. Married John Van Evera, of Davenport, Iowa. Occupation, dairyman and insurance agent. Issue: (1) Raymond, (2) Gertrude, (3) Arthur, (4) Jay.

NEWTON W. CESSNA, (VII), Thomas R., (VI).

Born August 13, 1857. Occupation, retired farmer. Address, Grinnell, Iowa. Married Nannie Skiles, of Walcott, Iowa. Issue: (1) Pearl, (2) Ruby (dec), (3) Maud.

BELLE CESSNA, (VII), Thomas R., (VI).

Address, Wellman, Iowa. Born September 17, 1860. Married Weller Robinson, of Montpelier, Iowa. Occupation, stock breeder. Issue: (1) Joy, (2) Genevera.

JOHN T. CESSNA, (VII), Thomas R., (VI).

Born October 27, 1862. Occupation, traveling collector. Address, Grinnell, Iowa. Married Elsie Brown, of Mason City, Iowa. Issue: (1) Gladys, (2) Blythe, (3) Thomas R., (4) Mildred.

HATTIE CESSNA, (VII), Thomas R., (VI).

Address, Webster City, Iowa. Born November 25, 1863. Married Alfred Jacobs. Occupation, merchant. Issue (1) Ethelwyn, (2) Claire.

MYRTLE CESSNA, (VII), Thomas R., (VI).

Address, Boston, Mass. Born November 27, 1866. Married Frank Porage, of Newton, Iowa. Occupation, minister.

CHRISTIANA CESSNA VI, William v, John iv

Address, Enid, Fulton County, Pa. Married William L. Cunningham. Occupation, teacher; later, farmer. Issue: (1) William, (2) Homer, (3) George (died young), (4) Rachel, (5) Anna, (6) John, (7) Reuben, (8) Myrtle, (9) Harry, (10) Jessica.

WILLIAM CUNNINGHAM, (VII), Christiana, (VI).

Address, Enid, Pa. Occupation, County Commissioner and farmer. Age, about 42. Married Minerva Griffith. Issue: (1) Frank, (2) Daniel.

HOMER CUNNINGHAM, (VII), Christiana, (VI).

Married Laura Stoner. Issue: (1) Mac, (2) Helen, (3) Sybel (died young), (4) William, (5) Myrtle.

Homer Cunningham was a bright and active lawyer, practiced law in Chicago, Ill., and died there, aged 38.

RACHEL CUNNINGHAM, (VII), Christiana, (VI).

Address, Enid, Pa. Married Harry Edwards, a merchant. Issue: (1) Marian, (2) Laura, (3) Reed.

ANNA CUNNINGHAM, (VII), Christiana, (VI).

Address 87½ Boylsom Street, Bradford, Pa. Married Julius Rhaesa. Issue: (1) Julius, (2) Louisa.

JOHN CUNNINGHAM, (VII), Christiana, (VI).

Address, Hastings, Iowa. Occupation, supervisor of hospital. Not married, age, 33.

REUBEN CUNNINGHAM, (VII), Christiana, (VI).

Address, Olean, New York. Age 31. Occupation, merchant. Married Laura Morgan.

MYRTLE CUNNINGHOM, (VII), Christiana. (VI).

Address, Viroqua, Ill. Married Mancil Pollard.

HARRY CUNNINGHAM, (VII), Christiana, (VI).

Address, Medico Chi., Philadelphia, Pa. Student Age, about 28. Single.

JESSICA CUNNINGHAM, (VII), Christiana, (VI).

Address, Clearville, Pa. Single. Occupation, school teacher.

RACHEL CESSNA VI, Williim v, John iv

Married Reuben Smith, whose address is Charlesville, Pa. Occupation, retired farmer and stockman. Issue. (1) Lilly (died young), (2) John C., (3) Carrie R., (4) Clayton.

JOHN C. SMITH, (VII), Rachel, (VI).

Occupation, supervisor of P. R. R. Co. Address, Washington, D. C. Single. Age, 40.

CARRIE R. SMITH, (VII), Rachel, (VI).

Address, Bellwood, Pa. Married, Sylvester Cessna, an employee of P. R. R. Co. Issue: (1) Leota, (2) Mary.

CLAYTON SMITH, (VII), Rachel, (VI).

Married Miss Hastings, from Lancaster County, Pa. Address, Charlesville, Pa.

REBECCA CESSNA VI, William V.

Married Josiah Smith. Issue: (1) M. B., who married Amanda Wertz . (2) Reuben, who married Miss Gordon. (3) Mary, who married Levi Hardman. (4) Martha, who married William Whipp. (5) Joe, who married Miss Smith. (6) Rachel, who married Mr. Fisher, (7) William, who married Miss Whetstone. (8) Fred, who married Miss Diehl. (9) Ruth, who married Rev. H. McClintock. (10) Clara, who married Harvey Elder. (11) Laura, who married George Sleiger.

The following was taken from the Bedford (Pa.) Inquirer:

Mrs. Rebecca E. Smith was born in Friend's Cove, Bedford County,

March 23, 1824, died April 10, 1903, aged 79 years and 18 days. Her maiden name was Cessna. She was united in marriage with Josiah Smith, on the 7th day of October, 1841. Her husband preceded her 32 years ago to the spirit world. She was left with a family of eleven children, five sons and six daughters, all of whom survive her, and all are living within a radius of a few miles of the old home, except Mrs. H. J. Elder, who resides in Terra Hautte, Indiana, and Mrs. Rev. H. McClintock, of Ohio City, Ohio. She was a member of the Lutheran church for sixty years, and was a faithful follower of the blessed Master. She was a kind, loving mother, always ready to lend a helping hand to her family and all others. She was a kind neighbor and always ready to assist the poor and needy. She was held in high esteem in the community in which she lived as was verified by the large concourse of relatives, friends and neighbors that followed her to her last resting place. She was an intense sufferer for the past ten years, but she bore her sufferings patiently, always looking to higher power for strength and comfort during her illness. All was done for her that her children and kind friends could do. The funeral sermon was preached by her pastor, Rev. Jones, from the text—"Be ye also ready." Our loss is her eternal gain.

J. BOONE CESSNA VI. William v. see p. 54

Address, Hastings, Neb. Married Katharine Brown, of Erie, Pa., June 12, 1872. Issue: (1) W. Brown, (2) Reon B., who is six feet four inches tall.

Rachel Cessna IV, John III.

Married Mr. Williams. Lived and died in Cumberland Valley, Bedford County, Pa. Issue: Hannah, who married James Haney; John, who went to Ohio; Margaret, who married John Hammer March 5, 1809; Polly, who married Mr. Norris and lived near Hancock, Md.; Sarah, who married Sam Smith and lived in Friend's Cove; Nellie, who married Mr. Ressler and died near Rainsburg; Elizabeth, who married Mr. Wertz, of Cumberland Valley; Rebecca, who married Mr. Simmons and lived in Ohio; Rachel, who married Mr. McCoy and lived in Ohio.

SARAH WILLIAMS V, RACHEL IV.

Married Sam Smith and lived in Friend's Cove. Issue: William, died in Cumberland Valley; Anthony, died in Napier township; Henry W., lived in Cumberland Valley; Hannah, married Mr. Arnold.

MARGARET P. WILLIAMS V, RACHEL IV.

Born February 25, 1789, died March 2, 1846. Married John Hammer March 5, 1809. Issue: (1) Rachel W., born February 22, 1810, died September 11, 1850. (2) Tobias, born September 22, 1811. (3) John W., born December 13, 1813, died January 30, 1814. (4) Josiah, born December 26, 1814, died July 13, 1815. (5) James H., born March 11, 1816, died February 5, 1817. (6) Thomas B., born January 3, 1818, died January 16, 1857. (7) Maria, born September 11, 1820. (8) John W., born December 11, 1822, died October 18, 1865. (9) Margaret A., born April 4, 1825, died July 12, 1899. (10) Malinda M., born April 15, 1827, died May 6, 1829. (11) Elmira L., born February 10, 1829, died March 23, 1830. (12) Jackson, born May 15, 1831, died January 13, 1833.

MARGARET A. HAMMER. vi, Margaret P. v.

Married S. Morgan Reno, of Columbus City, Iowa. Issue: (1) Margaret A., born April 4, 1825. (2) Charles M., born June 1, 1840. (3) Flora M., born December 10, 1851.

MARIA HAMMER vi, Margaret v.

Address, Iowa City, Iowa. Miss Hammer writes that she was a member of the Western Sanitary Commission and for her services in caring for the sick and wounded during the Civil War she now receives a pension. In such service she states she has traveled a great deal. She was in the

63

South in its day of beauty and saw it later in the reverse.

The following is an account of the death of Mrs. Margaret Reno as printed in local paper, Iowa City, Iowa:

Mrs. Margaret A. Reno has gone to that "undiscovered country from whose bourn no traveler returns." This noble woman, after performing the manifold duties of a long and useful career, has put aside life's burdens and sought that eternal rest which is promised those mothers of Israel who make the world better and happier for their living in it.

Mrs. Reno was past 74 years of age, having been born in Schellsburg, Bedford County, Pennsylvania, April 4, 1825. She came to Burlington, Iowa, in 1839. In 1843 she was married to Morgan Reno, at Columbus City, Iowa, and the same year they settled in Iowa City, where they lived continuously until the grim visitor bade them labor no more. Mrs. Reno was widely known by our pioneers and though not slavishly bending her knee to the tyranny of society, held a rank second to none in the social circles of this city and Johnson County. Indeed, Mr. and Mrs. Reno held a foremost place in the social world of the State for Mr. Reno was the last of the Territorial Treasurers of Iowa, and the first State Treasurer of this Commonwealth. He was also Mayor of Iowa City in 1857.

For long years, Mrs. Reno was connected with Trinity church. While strength was given her she was actively allied with the interests and good works of that institution, and though, in late years, power to energetically participate was taken away, her heart beat warm for the cause and her hopes and prayers were with it ever.

Her hand found much to do in lightening the burdens and lifting the bowed down hearts of others. Gentle and strengthening sympathy she always had for the grieving, while to the plea of the deserving needy she never turned a deaf ear, even though great riches were never given her to carry on all the works of charity to which her heart inclined.

Mrs. Reno passed away Wednesday, July 12, at 2.40 p. m. She had been ill a year and a half, though bed-ridden but a few weeks. The funeral services were conducted by Rev. Dr. George Watson, at her late home, 528 North Dubuque street, at 4 o'clock, Friday, July 14. Mrs. Reno is survived by a devoted son and daughter, ex-Mayor Charles M. Reno and Mrs. W. F. (Flora) Hohmann. Miss Maria L. Hammer, her sister, is now the sole survivor of twelve children.

Unostentatious and unassuming, a beautiful simplicity crowned Mrs. Reno's character, and when she "wrapped the drapery of her couch about her and lay down to pleasant dreams," one of the best of women and noblest of mothers bade farewell to the scenes of a well-spent earthly life. Like a lovely jewel in the rich casket of memory, thoughts of her shall endure for aye. Those who knew her best loved her most, and to those who came in daily contact with her peaceful and yet exalted life, something of its sweetness and nobility has been unconsciously imparted and shall abide with them forever.

Tobias Hammer died at Leon, Iowa, leaving one daughter, Jessie, now Mrs. Finley.

Thomas Hammer was murdered by Mexicans January 16, 1857.

Morgan C. Reno, son of Charles M. Reno, born August 18, 1871. When only seventeen months old in company with his mother and uncle travelled some sixty miles on the night of December 23, 1872, when the thermometer was 33 degrees below zero.

JOHN WILLIAM HAMMER vi. Margaret v.

Killed in South America in 1865. Was Captain of a steamboat that operated on the Rivers Orinoco and Apure. The steamer was called "Apure." He was also agent for a line of steamers incorporated in the city of New York known as the "Orinoco Steam Navigation Company." A monument was erected in Bolivar City, Venezuela, to his memory for courage and bravery in caring for women and children on board his boat when attacked by insurgents. A meeting of all the Consuls was called, including the leading nations of the world and strong resolutions adopted condemning the killing of Captain Hammer. I have in my possession copy of resolution.

The following obituary of James A. Jackson is taken from a Sioux City, Iowa, paper:

The funeral of the late James A. Jackson was held at 3 o'clock yesterday afternoon at the family residence at Morning Side. The remains were taken to Council Bluffs on the 6.25 train last evening. The funeral was a very large one. The cars on the elevated were crowded to their capacity for over an hour before the time for the services. There were several hundred people present, including the representative business and professional men of the city. It is seldom that so large a number of the city's pioneers has been together as gathered yesterday to pay the last tribute of respect to the memory of one who had been a leader among them. The funeral was conducted by Rev. George H. Cornell, after the forms of the Episcopal church. A quartette provided the singing. The pall bearers were A. S. Garretson, E. C. Peters, John P. Allson, Adam V. Larimer, C. G. Culver and W. H. Myers. The remains were accompanied to Council Bluffs by a large party. It included Rev. and Mrs. George H. Cornell, W. H. Myers, E. C. Peters, George Snook, A. S. Wilson and wife, Miss Wilson and Miss Lizzie Wilson, Mrs. James A. Jackson, Mr. and Mrs. A. M. Jackson and son, Jimmie; A. V. Larimer, Mrs. Record, of Glenwood, sister of the deceased, and her son, James Record. The remains will be taken in charge at Council Bluffs by the Masons, of which order Mr. Jackson was a member. The funeral there will be held at 2 o'clock this afternoon, and the letters and telegrams received here indicate that it will be one of the largest ever seen in the city.

65

There are few men in the west who are better known than was James A. Jackson. He was a pioneer of pioneers. In half a dozen western States are great cities which he helped to found. He has been actively and very extensively engaged in numerous lines of business during a series of years extending over the last third of a century. He will be mourned not only by those who knew him as one of the most enterprising, progressive and public spirited citizens of Sioux City, but also by those who knew him as a pioneer and leader in the development of Omaha, Council Bluffs, St. Joseph, St. Louis, Denver, Salt Lake, and other western cities. He was one of the founders of the State of Nebraska, and helped lay the foundation of the great cattle industry, which is now the source of a large part of the wealth of Colorado and Wyoming.

Mr. Jackson was born in Ohio in 1829. His family was from Virginia and was one of the old families of that State. Mr. Jackson was an own cousin of John Cessna, of Pennsylvania, who died a few days ago, and who made himself famous in political annals as the leader of the "Grant 306" in the National Republican Convention of 1880. While he was still very young his father died and he removed with his mother to Missouri. Theirs was the first white family to settle on what was then known as the Platte reservation; and they were the first white people to live on the site of what is now the city of St. Joseph. Mr. Jackson lived here on a farm until he was 15 years of age, when he entered the employ of Milton Tootle. A few years after the firm of Tootle & Jackson was organized, and established houses in St. Joseph, Council Bluffs, Omaha, Sioux City and Lewis, Iowa. Mr. Jackson went to Council Bluffs as one of its pioneer settlers. He married there a stepdaughter of Dr. Cook, with whom he was associated in founding the city of Sioux City. Mr. Jackson was one of a group of thirteen men who laid out the original town plot of the city of Omaha. He was the youngest of the number and the last to survive. His death removes, therefore, the last of the little company of men recognized as the founders of Omaha. Mr. Jackson built the first brick house in the territory of Nebraska. It was for a long time used as the capitol of the territory.

Although at this period he lived at Council Bluffs, Mr. Jackson assisted Dr. Cook in his pioneer efforts at founding Sioux City. He brought to Sioux City the first frame building ever erected here. It was occupied by the firm of Tootle & Jackson, and until a year or two ago, when it was burned, stood at the corner of Second and Pearl streets and was known as one of the landmarks of the city. In 1865 Mr. Jackson moved from Council Bluffs to St. Louis, where for a number of years he conducted the largest wholesale grocery in the city. He remained there until 1876, when he removed with his son, A. M. Jackson, to Leadville, Colo. Here they associated themselves together in business for the first time and were transfer agents for the Atchison, Topeka and Santa Fe Railroad, besides conducting a wholesale grocery business. During his residence in Leadville Mr. Jackson organized the Evans-Jackson Live Stock Company, the first company of its kind in the State of Wyoming. He continued in the cattle business until 1888, when he came to Sioux City. During the period of his residence in Colorado he became extensively interested in Salt Lake and Denver, in both of which cities he is still well known.

He removed from Leadville to Sioux City and engaged in the real estate business. He was a leader in founding the suburb of Morning Side. The property which he had handled there has been in the same family ever since it was originally entered by Dr. Cook, to whom the original government patent was issued.

Mr. Jackson's business career in Sioux City is known to everybody

66

here. He has been one of the most extensive and successful dealers in real estate, and a leader in public enterprises of every character. In everything that has occupied his attention he has met uniform success, and in his death the city loses one of the men who contributed much toward building the city of Sioux City on the cite of what had been the village of Sioux City.

STATEMENT OF HON. JOHN CESSNA

Dictated by Hon. John Cessna, of Bedford, Pa., a few weeks before his death in 1893.

It is a part of the history of the Cessna family, that John Cessna was a Huguenot and was in the battle of the Boyne in 1690. In that year he married an Irish girl and came to America, settling in eastern Pennsylvania. He raised a family and among these was a son, John. He too had a family and located somewhere near Shippensburg, Pa., and raised quite a large family; among these were John, Charles, et. al. Of this family John was the great-grandfather of myself. This family is repeatedly mentioned in the Pennsylvania Archives and Colonial Records. This John Cessna held office in Bedford County prior to the Revolution. One of the family was prosecuted for some irregularity in supplying provisions for the army. I think this was Charles. He was tried and acquitted. John became somewhat prominent and noted as a patriot. In 1774 he was chosen a delegate from Bedford County to a convention to frame a Constitution for the State of Pennsylvania. Of this convention 'Benjamin Franklin was president, and it resulted in the production of the Constitution of 1776. This John Cessna was three times elected Sheriff of Bedford County—1789-91-93. (The term of the office at that time was but two years.) At the time of his death he left in his desk, or office, large bundles of continental money. He came up from Shippensburg in 1765 and purchased the farm in Friend's Cove still occupied by his descendants; this he purchased from William MacClay afterwards United States

Senator from Pennsylvania. From the day on which he purchased until the present time, this farm remains in the family. This John Cessna raised a family of 13 children. His wife died when he was 70 years of age. He then married a young woman and raised five more children. The late Sheriff Cessna was the oldest son of the youngest son of these five children.

The late James Cessna, of Cumberland Valley, was the youngest of this family. Among the children was one named John, a son of the first wife; at the death of his father the farm was appraised and taken by him. He, too, raised a family of 12 or 13 children. He named three of his sons John; all of whom died young. He had, however, two other sons, William and Samuel. The latter was the late Judge Cessna and the former was William Cessna, a farmer of Colerain township and father of myself. The third boy named John was living when William and Samuel were born and named. John, the father of William and Samuel, did not live to a very old age and after his death his farm was taken at an appraisement by his son, William, in 1819. William lived until 1865 and left the farm by will to two of his sons, George and William. George released or conveyed his share of the farm to William, who still lives upon it, raising a family.

John Cessna, my grandfather, married Mary McCauslin; she is reported to have been a very beautiful Irish girl who came from Ireland when she was but six months old and was also the mother of 12 or 13 children. Among these were William and Samuel, as above referred to, the only male survivors; Sally, who married George James; Rachel, who married a Mr. Rogers and had two children, he dying, she married a Mr. Jackson and raised quite a large family, and died recently a widow of high character and prominence at Council Bluffs, Iowa; Elizabeth, who married Peter Morgart, of Friend's Cove, (she, too, was the mother of a large family); Ellen married Rev. Casten and had three or four children, after his death she married Thomas C. McCavern. They moved to Denver, Col., and left a family

HON. JOHN CESSNA.
Pages 45 to 54.

69

and are now located in Helena or Butte, Montana. One of these was the wife of the Territory Auditor and he afterwards became a State officer.

The members of these different families are scattered all over the States of the Union. They were generally vigorous, much respected, and useful people. None of them being especially distinguished or prominent.

Among the children of John Cessna of the Convention of 1774 were Elizabeth Vicroy, of Cumberland Valley. She died at the age of 89 years; Rachel Williams, a widow, who died at the age of 91 years; Jonathan, who died at 93 years of age in the early part of 1853 in Cumberland Valley. He had a son, Jonathan, who became Judge of the Courts of Harden County, Ohio,—a township of that county is named after him; Stephen, who lived and died in Perry County, Pa., aged about 95. Stephen's descendants reside in that county mostly. One of them was a Senator in the State of Florida. (This I take to be a mistake, believing the Florida Senator to be Hon. W. K. Cessna, of Gainsville, Florida, a descendant of William Cessna, who lived at Buffalo Mills, Pa—Ed.) Jonathan Cessna, of Harden County, Ohio, had a son, William, who was several times a member of the Ohio Legislature and also a son who was a prominent physician— was a physician for the P. R. R. Co., for the District of Northwestern Ohio. One of the name was at one time Adjutant General of the State of Indiana; another was Sheriff of Kosciusco County, Indiana; another was a Judge in one of the counties of Kentucky.

They are scattered over all Western States of the Union. As already stated, Mrs. Rachel Jackson raised a large and highly respected family, some of whom are prominent in Iowa and California. Her granddaughter is now the wife of Judge Wilson, President Law Judge of four counties in Kansas.

The biography of myself is pretty well known in the State. The Legislative Record at the close of the session of 1863 contains a number of speeches in regard to my ability as a parliamentarian and my success as a presiding

70

officr, which I prize very highly. As the Records of the State, proceedings of Convention—State and National—are all now accessible, nothing further is added on these subjects.

It is matter of much regret that the conversations between people now living and some of the earlier members of the family have not been preserved. Jonathan Cessna, Stephen Cessna, Mrs. Vicroy and Rachel Williams could have given definite and accurate information which would have thrown much light on the subject.

William Cessna, of Buffalo Mills, has not been named as a member of this family. He was, however, a son of John Cessna of 1776, lived long, was a highly respected citizen of Harrison township, Bedford County, Pa., raised a family and died at a good old age.

BIOGRAPHY OF HON. JOHN CESSNA

(Bedford County History, published 1884.)

Hon. John Cessna was born in Colerain township, Bedford County, Pa., June 29, 1821. His great-grandfather, whose name was also John, was a member of the convention which framed the Constitution of 1776. He served three terms of two years each as Sheriff of Bedford County, having been chosen to said office in 1789-1791-1793; and likewise served as Major of Bedford county troops during the Revolutionary War. The grandfather of the latter, also named John Cessna, came to Pennsylvania in 1690, a Huguenot seeking freedom and liberty. In 1842 John Cessna, the subject of this article, graduated from Marshall College, at Lancaster, Pa. He has been president of the board of trustees of this institution since the resignation of James Buchanan, in 1865, having been re-elected unanimously each year since. In 1844 he was tutor of the Latin language in his alma mater. In 1848 he was a member of

the revenue board of Pennsylvania by appointment of Judge
Black. He served as a member of the Pennsylvania House
of Representatives in 1850, 1851, 1862 and 1863; was
Speaker of the same legislative body in 1851 and again in
1863, receiving at the end of each term a unanimous vote of
thanks, every member present voting to compliment his
integrity, fairness and ability as a speaker. During his two
terms as Speaker no appeal was ever entered, and conse-
quently no decision reversed, which indicates the scope of
his accurate knowledge of parlimentary law.

He was elected to the 41st Congress in 1868 and again
in 1872 to the 43rd Congress. There he was frequently
called upon to preside over that body as Speaker pro tem,
and in committee of the whole. During the memorable and
important contest over the civil rights bill, Speaker Blaine
deputized him to take the chair, which he occupied through
a whole night and on all the many occasions of such service
no appeal was ever taken from his decisions.

To be worthy the confidence of the great Speaker, Mr.
Blaine, and to be trusted with the mighty interests of the
Republican party on that momentous occasion when
"human rights" and the sacred promise of his party were at
stake, was a great honor, which this distinguished leader of
his party extended to Mr. Cessna. Doubtless there is no
public man in the State of Pennsylvania who has not met
him in national conventions, where he was always a prominent figure, and his parliamentary skill and wisdom frequently guided those bodies quietly and safely to peace,
good order and harmony. Thus, as a member, has he attended national conventions which met at Cincinnati in
1856, at Charleston and Baltimore in 1860, at Chicago in
1868, at Cincinnati in 1876, and at Chicago in 1880.

In his career as a lawyer he has shown marked ability
and integrity. After reading law in the office of Hon.
Samuel M. Barclay, of Bedford, Pa., he was admitted to the
bar June 25, 1845. Since that time he has been in active
practice in Bedford, Fulton and Franklin counties, and oc-
casionally in Blair, Somerset, Huntingdon and other coun-

72

ties, and in the Supreme Court of the State. He has attended every session of the latter court held for his district since 1848, except two—once by reason of illness and once when his duties as member of Congress prevented. The many volumes of Pennsylvania's State reports are also a monument to Mr. Cessna's skill and ability as a lawyer. He has been executor, administrator, trustee and guardian for more than two hundred people, and in but one case was there an exception filed to his accounts, and that was withdrawn and costs paid by the party making it. In 1865 in the convention which nominated Gen. Hartranft for Auditor General, the Hon. Thaddeus Stevens moved in open convention that Hon. John Cessna be made Chairman of the State Central Committee, which was done, and the State ticket was elected by over 22,000 majority, carrying every doubtful district in the State, legislative and senatorial.

Again, in 1880, as Chairman of the Republican State Committee of Pennsylvania he distinguished himself. At an early stage he recognized the importance of securing the vote of Indiana for Garfield, and amid the claims of the Democracy as to their ability to carry Pennsylvania he announced that Indiana and Ohio should be the first care of the Keystone State, and while he organized his own he earnestly urged the prime importance of making a certainty of those spoken of, and by great perseverance secured the aid which largely tended to accomplish desired results in those States. So valuable were his services in that direction that the Secretary of the Indiana State Committee, the Hon. W. H. H. Terrell, in a letter dated October 30, 1880, addressed to Gen. James A. Elkin, late of Pittsburg, recognized his services in these words: "Glorious John Cessna 'held up our hands' with material aid, as if Indiana was in his own bailiwick. While others lacked faith in our ability to carry Indiana at the State election, John Cessna stood by us manfully and bravely."

Among the records of the Republican State Committee is another letter, from the Hon. John C. New, Chairman of the Republican State Committee of Indiana, which is addressed to "Hon. John Cessna," and says: "My dear sir, in acknowledging the receipt of your communication of the 28th inst., I desire first to say, that my thanks are due to you dating from the opening day of this campaign to to-day, for your hearty co-operation, generous sympathy and daily evidences of your intention to not only take excellent good care of Pennsylvania, but to give to Indiana the strongest help you could command. I have received from you more assistance and more evidence of interest in our campaign work than from any man east of the Alleghenies, and Indiana stands to-day under obligations to Hon. John Cessna."

As a Republican politician his views are broader than the confines of his own State, and as Chairman of the Republican State Committee he not only moored Pennsylvania safely by a splendid majority in the harbor of a nation, but he reached out and was largely instrumental in placing the whole northern fleet alongside the Keystone.

Besides having attended most assiduously to his professional duties and the many public trusts imposed upon him, Mr. Cessna has also devoted much attention to the development of the resources of his native county, and the building of needed avenues of commerce. He was a leading spirit during the inception and construction of the Bedford and Bridgeport Railroad, and since 1870 has served as president of the company. He has likewise been active in advancing the interests of the proposed new trunk line of railway, known as the South Pennsylvania or Harrisburg and Western, which, leading from Harrisburg westward, will intersect centrally from east to west, the counties of Bedford and Somerset, as well as others on the southern border of the State. In brief his record as a citizen, lawyer and public official sufficiently indicates even to the most negligent observers of passing events that he is a gentleman possessing superior ability and an untarnished reputation—one who has ever enjoyed the confidence and respect of those composing the community in which he resides, as well as the esteem and admiration of the people of counties surrounding him.

He was married at Mercersburg, Pa., September 24,

1844, by John W. Nevin, D. D., to Miss Ellen J. Shaffer, daughter of Daniel Shaffer, Esq., of that place. They commenced housekeeping in Bedford in the fall of that year, and have resided there ever since. They have five living children, three sons and two daughters, having buried one son and one daughter many years since.

The following articles were taken from some of the daily papers at the time of Hon. John Cessna's death:

From the Philadelphia Public Ledger.

BEDFORD, Pa., Dec.13.—Ex-Congressman John Cessna died at 11 o'clock to-night of diabetes insipidus,i n his 72d year. Mr. Cessna had been in bad health for the past three months. In fact his illness dates back to the closing hours of the last Legislature, where, both on the floor and in the committee rooms, he was an untiring worker.

For the past two days every citizen has been earnestly inquiring after the health of the venerable state-man, yet, while this is being written, not half a dozen persons outside of his own family, his physicians and the newspaper men, know that "Uncle John," as he was known by every person in the county, both old and young, for over half a century, is lying cold in death.

About six weeks ago Mr. Cessna went to New York on a business errand against the advice of his physician, and, with one or two exceptions, he has not left his home since. He has been constantly surrounded by his family during the past two weeks, but not until this week have they realized that his condition was serious. The funeral will take place on Saturday.

John Cessna has been a commanding and interesting figure in Pennsylvania and national politics for 40 years. Few men have continued actively in public affairs to such a late period in life, and few have enjoyed such uninterrupted popularity.

He was born in Colerain township, Bedford County, June 29, 1821. His early education was received in the common schools. After exhausting their facilities he entered the Military Academy at Bedford, and then became a student at Marshall College, Mercersburg, from which he graduated September, 1842. During the next two years he was Latin tutor in the college, and was also engaged in the study of law. In June, 1845, he was admitted to the Bedford County Bar. He was a State Revenue Commissioner in 1848. He was appointed by Judge Black, and was at the time 26 years of age. His district was composed of Somerset, Bedford, Blair and Franklin. This appointment had no political significance. During the sessions of 1850-1851 he was a member of the House of Representatives, and again from 1860 to 1863, and was Speaker in 1851 and 1863. He was a member of the Forty-first and Forty-third Congresses, serving on the Committee on Elections and the War Department. In the Forty-third Congress he was a member of the Judiciary Committee, of which Benjamin F. Butler was Chairman.

When the deceased entered upon his political career he was a Democrat. The first National Democratic Convention he attended was at Cincinnati, in May, 1856, when James Buchanan was nominated for the Presidency. Mr. Cessna was Secretary of the Pennsylvania State delegation. He was not friendly to Buchanan's Kansas-Nebraska policy. Mr. Cessna

was a delegate to the Charleston Convention, which assembled in April,
1860, and made a motion to appoint all the committees at once and pre-
scribing the method of so doing. This was adopted by four-fifths of the
convention. He was then made Chairman of the Committee on Organization and Rules and supported Douglass throughout. John A. Logan was
a member of this convention as a delegate from Illinois, and then began a
friendship between Cessna and Logan, which remained unshaken until
Logan's death. At the first meeting of the Committee on Organization
a motion to abolish the unit rule was lost by two votes. Notice was given
to Cessna that two of the three members of the committee who voted to
sustain the unit rule motion were willing to change their votes. Between
two and three o'clock Cessna notified the committee to reassemble, and
soon after the former vote was reconsidered, and a motion to rescind the
unit rule adopted. The committee's action was sustained by the convention and Douglas gained many votes in consequence, and made him the
Democratic candidate for the Presidency. Mr. Cessna remained in the
Charleston Convention until it went to Baltimore, and there also Cessna
went and stayed until the final adjourment. The Charleston Convention
was most exciting, owing to the sectional feeling that then existed. War
spirit was then on the rise, and every man held pronounced views on the
slavery question. Cessna was within a few feet of Yancey when he
seceded from the convention, and that night the former heard speeches
from the balcony of the Mills House that predicted that "the pen was nibbed
to write the history of the Southern Confederacy." Party feeling ran high
and the excitement was intense. The Mills House speeches made the
Douglas men firmer in their determination to prevent the enforcement of
the unit rule. When the Rebellion broke out Mr. Cessna became a Republican. In 1868 he was a delegate to the Republican National Convention
at Chicago, and joined in the unanimous vote for the nomination of General Grant. He next attended the Convention of 1876, which nominated
Rutherford B. Hayes. At this convention he was Chairman of the Committee on Rules. Mr. Cessna was a delegate to the Republican National
Convention of 1880, and served on the Committee on Credentials, in which
an interesting contest took place. In relating his experience on this occasion, Mr. Cessna said:

"The committee was in session three days and two entire nights, and
during that time I never in my life heard such eloquent speeches, or such
profound reasoning. In no court of justice have I ever heard more able
speeches or more powerful arguments than were there made. Nor was all
this confined to one side; each element exhibited marked intellectual
strength. Emory Storrs, of Chicago, made a great outburst of oratory
and argument. So also did General Tracy, of New York, and the late
Secretary Chandler. Green B. Raum, of Illinois, was another eloquent
speaker. I am not afraid to say that I was one of the 300 that stood up
solidly for Grant. As everybody knows, Garfield was nominated, and I
was made one of the State Committee appointed to conduct his campaign
in Pennsylvania. Of all the national conventions I attended, that at
Charleston was the most exciting, by all means, owing to the sectional
issues then prevailing. I think that for ability, argument, oratory and
prolonged interest the Convention of 1880, that nominated Garfield, was
the most memorable."

The deceased was a member of many State Conventions, in fact, he was
very rarely absent on such occasions, and, when present, was influential,
through his incisive speeches and skillful persuasion, in moulding the
action of these bodies. In February, 1860, he was a member of the Democratic State Convention which was held at Reading and which nominated

Foster for Governor. The convention was memorable in Pennsylvania politics as being the first which placed a tariff plank in its platform. This portion of the platform was in part prepared by Mr. Cessna and was by him reported to the convention.

The Republican Convention of 1865, by which General Hartranft was nominated for Auditor General, appointed Mr. Cessna member of the State Central Committee. He became the Chairman of the Committee and conducted the following campaign with the utmost vigor, resulting in Hartranft's election by a large majority under the conditions which then prevailed. He was also Chairman of the Republican State Committee in 1880. While a member of the Pennsylvania Legislature in the war period, in 1862 and 1863, he earnestly supported every war measure of the Government. In 1875 he was appointed Assistant Attorneyy General of the United States, but declined. He has been President of Franklin and Marshall College, at Lancaster, since 1865, and is at present a member of the Pennsylvania House of Representatives.

From Harper's Weekly, Dec. 30, 1893.

An active public life of nearly fifty years' continuous duration ended on the 13th inst., when John Cessna died in his lifetime home at Bedford, Pennsylvania. When "Uncle John," as politicians and newspaper men liked to call him, first held office—a commissioership of revenue—people were still "staging it" across his native State of Pennsylvania; and Dickens's Notes, in which he described his drive across the old "camel-back" bridge at Harrisburg, was a late addition to many Pennsylvania libraries, in which that particular passage was marked. And only last spring, on the last right of the Legislature's session, the member from Bedford was vigorously and successfully fignting the efforts of the trolley companies of Philadelphia and Pittsburg to plant their squeaky standards in every highway in the State.

A long and useful life lay between. Mr. Cessna was a thorough-going politician of the old swallow-tailed Buchanan school, which viewed with something of wonder, not to say contempt, a man who saw a field of political activity outside of the ranks of the two great parties. But he had a high personal standard, which he stuck to and held up, and so passed spotless through an era of politics in which the Pennsylvania public man who remained uncorrupt did so through inherent integrity of character. He was the son of a Bedford County farmer, and was graduated from Marshall College. Mercersburg, in 1842. He was admitted to the bar in 1845, and immediately became active on the Democratic side of politics, with such energy and ability that the year 1850 saw him, in his thirtieth year, Speaker of the Pennsylvania House. As a delegate to the National Convention in 1856 he aided in the nomination of James Buchanan, and continued to act with the dominant faction in the Democratic party until 1861, when he was elected to the House as a Union Democrat. He remained in the old faith till 1863, when his high character and unimpeachable patriotism made him, as Speaker once more of the House, an invaluable supporter of Governor Curtin in his historic efforts to put forth the whole resources of the greatest of the border States for the suppression of the rebellion. In the same year his Union and anti-slavery sentiments led him at last into active membership of the Republican party, which always thereafter delighted to honor him. He was Chairman of the State Committee in 1865, a post in which he had been immediately preceded by A. K. McClure and Wayne MacVeagh. He was, in 1868, a delegate to the convention which nominated Grant. In that year, and again in 1872, he was elected to Congress, and in 1876 helped to nominate General Hayes. In 1880 he was one of the famous "306" w..o voted continuously for Grant, but, like a loyal partisan, he went home and, as Chairman of the State Committee, set about the successful creation of the regular majority for his leader's successful opponent. His re.urn to ...e Legislature last winter was after an absence of many years. He was seventy-two years old, and died of diabetes. He was a kindly man whom every one knew and liked, and there is no hamlet in the great State he served so long where there will not be some one who feels a personal bereavement .n the death of "Uncle John."

From the Johnstown ' ribune.

The death of Hon. John Cessna, of Bedford, will be learned with sorrow by all who had the pleasure of his acquaintance, as well as by all others who have watched his course as an able, energetic worker in all good causes. Without disparagement to anybody, we believe he was the ablest, in general education, of any man in Pennsylvania. He was second to none in the country as a parliamentarian and statesman. He was a ready speaker, full of facts and arguments, and those who have seen him in national conventions, where great men only stood in the front, know he was as great as any one of them; we believe, take him all in all, he was greater than any one man in several Republican national conventions. The people of this district did not appear to know how big he was. Had he been less of a real Democrat, and put on frills, which many wear with not a tithe of his ability, he would likely have been taken nearer his true worth.

From the Chambersburg Public Opinion.

In the death of Hon. John Cessna Pennsylvania loses one of her most valued citizens. His career if not brilliant was ennobling. He was one of the men you would like for the enemies he made. Whether as lawyer, advocate, representative or friend, he could be relied upon. He was sincere and faithful in every relation.

The brief sketch given of him in another column shows a long and eventful career. He had a warm heart for Franklin County. Here it was that he received his collegiate education. Here he led to the altar the devoted one who share.. in his triumphs and sympathized with him in his sorrows. The "Greenspot" was a part of the old sixteenth district which sent him to the national halls of legislation. We, therefore, had a right to be proud of his achievements. It was natural he should have a warm side for us. A genial companion, a loyal friend, an educated Christian gentleman, of him it might be aptly said, he was a trusted educator of the mind and heart in all that was generous and ennobling. He had that rare combination, "a sound conscience for himself, with great tenderness for the consciences of other people."

"Why weep for him, who having won
    The bound of man's appointed years, at last,
Life's blessings all enjoyed, life's labors done,
    Serenely to his final rest has passed;
While the soft memory of his virtues yet
    Lingers like twilight hues, when the bright sun is set."

From the Philadelphia Press.

John Cessna, who died at Bedford yesterday was a man of varied political experience, and for more than forty years he was a very conspicuous figure in the affairs of Pennsylvania. During that time he has been a part of the history of both parties in the State. He spent very little of his time on the back seats.

He was a native of the county in which he always lived and where he died, for though he had changed his politics he was steadfast in his devotion to the people of Bedford, the most of whom knew him personally. Mr. Cessna began his public life as a revenue commissioner as far back as 1848, and two years later was a member of the lower house of the Legislature. He was twice Speaker of that body, once as a Democrat in 1851 and again as a Republican a dozen years later. Before the war he was a conspicuous figure in Democratic State and National conventions, and afterward equally conspicuous in the conventions of the Republican party. He helped to nominate Buchanan at Cincinnati in 1856, was a delegate to the Charleston Convention of 1860, when the Democratic party split, and eight years later he was at Chicago participating in the nomination of Grant. Twice, also, he served as Chairman of the Republican State Committee, and was twice a member of Congress.

In all these positions Mr. Cessna made himself felt as a man of force and ability. He was a leader in every position, and those qualities of leadership which had always distinguished him were quite as strongly displayed at the last session of the Legislature as at any former time, although he was then completing his 72d year. He had a quick and keen intelligence which gave him a natural advantage in discussion, and to this he added a courage which nothing daunted when he had once determined upon his course. He had given proof of this in many political controversies in this State, and during his brief service in Congress he was one of the most active and best known members. * * *

From a Bedford County paper.

In the death of Hon. John Cessna Bedford County suffers an irreparable loss, and the Keystone State is bereft of one who always took a great interest in her welfare. Few men reach the age he attained, living a life so active and useful, and leave the scene of action with such commendations of those who knew him as Mr. Cessna received. He served the people well in various capacities, being one of the most prominent members of the last house. His ringing denunciation of the combination of boss legislation in the closing hours of the session will always be a monument to his honesty, unselfishness and fearlessness.

He always had the best interests of his town at heart. It is seldom, if ever, that any public man has so endeared himself to the masses of the people. It has well been said by an exchange that "the cordial, endearing way public men at Harrisburg and all over the State had of speaking of 'Uncle John,' characterizes the widely known member from Bedford County. A stormy life in politics, extending to half a century, showed that Mr. Cessna could differ, and even differ from his own party, without incurring the hatred or enmity of any one. In this he furnishes a lesson to most politicians." At the bar, in the heat of the campaign—at all times, he held the highest esteem of all with whom he came in contact. His life is a model for the youth of the land. He had before him in early manhood a lofty ideal, and with steadfast eye and unwavering footsteps he surmounted all obstacles and reached the goal of his ambition.

Mr. Cessna's fame as a lawyer was not confined to his county nor to his State. He was a faithful, vigorous and clear-sighted legislator, both at the capital of the State and at the national capital.

The people of Bedford County, as well as the people of the commonwealth of Pennsylvania, sincerely mourn his death. They will ever cherish the memory of one who has served them so faithfully and well. The town of Bedford will always be proud of the honor this distinguished citizen has conferred upon her. He came to the end of his earthly career full of years and honors. His was a life well spent, and should be a guiding star to the young men who are fighting life's stern battle.

> "Lives of great men all remind us,
> We can make our lives sublime;
> And when dying leave behind us
> Footprints on the sands of time."

BIOGRAPHY OF J. B. CESSNA

(Taken from a History of Nebraska.)

J. B. Cessna, Attorney, Hastings, Nebraska, is a prominent member of the Adams County Bar, whose career has been both honorable and successful, is the subject of this sketch.

He was born in Bedford County, Pennsylvania, on the 24th day of March, 1840, and his parents, William and Rachel (Morgart) Cessna, were natives of the Keystone State. His father was born in 1800 and died in Bedford County at the age of sixty-four, the mother was born in 1789 and died in 1860. She was a prominent, leading and very consistent member of the Baptist Church—Old School—and was accustomed to write many articles for its papers and magazines. She was of German descent, while the father was of French and Huguenot.

Cessna's great-grandfather, whose name was John Cessna, was a member of the convention which framed the Constitution of Pennsylvania in 1776, he served three terms as Sheriff of Bedford County having been chosen to said office in 1779, 1781 and 1783 and likewise served as Major during the Revolutionary War and was subsequently with General Washington in suppressing the Whiskey Insurrection in Western Pennsylvania. The grandfather of the lat-

J. B. CESSNA.
Page 54.

81

ter came to Pennsylvania in 1690, a Huguenot seeking freedom and liberty.

J. B. Cessna is the youngest of eleven children, eight
of whom are still living. His brother, John, who died a
few years ago was a prominent politician of Pennsylvania
and was Speaker of the House of the Pennsylvania Legislature for three terms and three times represented the 18th
Congressional District in Congress. He was a prominent
politician for forty years and one of the leaders in politics in
that State for many years.

J. B. Cessna first attended the public schools of Pennsylvania and later "The Alleghany Male and Female Seminary" at Rainsburg, Pa. He entered the sophomore class at
Franklin and Marshall College at Lancaster, Pa., in September, 1861, and graduated from the same in July, 1864. One
year later he was admitted to the bar at Bedford, Pa., and
practiced law in that and other counties until April, 1885,
when he came to Hastings, Nebraska. He had a good practice in the counties of his native State and was admitted to
practice before the Supreme Court of the United States on
January 26, 1876, on motion of Hon. Jeremiah Black. He
was married to Miss Katharine Brown, of Erie, Pa., June 12,
1872, and thy have two children now living, W. Brown and
Reon B. W. Brown has been absent from home for several
years, has an important position with the Barber Asphalt
Paving Company with location at Detroit, Mich.

In politics J. B. Cessna adheres strictly to the Republican party. He is a member of the College Fraternity, Phi
Kapa Psi. He was admitted to practice before the Supreme
Court of Pennsylvania on May 15, 1868, and during his practice in that State he had quite a number of important cases
notably among which was the case of Noble vs. The Thomp-
son Oil Company. This case was in the courts for fifteen
years, was reversed by the Supreme Court of Pennsylvania
before Mr. Cessna became interested in it. On the third
argument a judgment obtained in the court below was unanimously affirmed; it was then taken to the Supreme Court of

the United States. Mr. Cessna was connected with the case as counsel for the plaintiff in the court below and defendant in error and in March, 1879, the case was decided in favor of the defendants in the Supreme Court of the United States by a divided court, four judges for affirmance and four against it; the court writing no opinion. The case involved $50,000 and was of great legal importance as many and intricate points were in controversy which were close and of intricate difficulty as indicated by the decision of the divided court. He was also concerned in another very important case in the oil regions between Thompson, Noble and Delemater, the amount involved was over $100,000.

Since coming west Mr. Cessna has had a good practice and here too has been employed in a number of important cases—the Keedle case contest in the United States Court of Private Land Claims to recover a very valuable tract of land in New Mexico worth several millions of dollars, as heirs of John G. Heath by virtue of a grant made to him by the Government of Mexico in 1821 under the reign of Iterbidie, was one of the most important cases of recent litigation; the parties whom he represented were successful in the first trial in the court below but subsequently lost. He was also attorney for C. L. Jones against the railway company in an interesting and important case in Illinois. This case was a suit to recover triple damages for illegal charges of freight under the railroad law of Illinois. The case resulted in a judgment in favor of plaintiff's claim, appeal was taken to the Supreme Court of the United States but the claim was paid before the case was reached for argument. Some forty or fifty similar cases were commenced in the court below, one or two were tried and verdict in favor of defendants, others were settled and compromised upon payment of costs; Jones was the only party who recovered judgment.

Mr. Cessna's specialty is land and equity suits, but he engages in a general practice, except the criminal business. He is an independent thinker, deriving his information, when practical, from original sources and is a hard working

S. ALBERT CESSNA.
Page 57.

84

industrious lawyer, always giving every question thorough and careful investigation, going to the bottom of every controverted question involved in the case in which he is concerned. He is a good, careful and reliable advisor and is generally successful in the cases in which he is interested, never encourages litigation without good reasons for success. ·

AUTOBIOGRAPHY OF S. A. CESSNA.

S. Albert Cessna was born near Rainsburg, County of Bedford, and State of Pennsylvania, on April 7, 1852. He received his education at the Rainsburg Seminary and was a teacher in that institution from 1876 to 1880. In 1881 he engaged in the mercantile business and continued in that pursuit for several years. He was appointed postmaster at Rainsburg by Postmaster General Thomas L. James during the Garfield administration and was re-commissioned by Postmaster General John Wanamaker on the 19th day of December, 1892, during the Harrison administration, served until November, 1893, when he was elected County Treasurer. The Everett Republican of February 5, 1897, says:

On Thursday of last week Mr. S. A. Cessna, the retiring County Treasurer, took the receipt of Charles Reiley, the incoming Treasurer, for $22,363.78, the amount found to be due the county from Mr. Cessna by the County Auditors, and the same day the full amount was turned over to Mr. Reiley in cash. The statement suggests the comment that Mr. Cessna has proved himself a careful and efficient public official, managing the many thousands of dollars of county funds that passed through his hands during his term of office without the loss of a penny. "Well done good and faithful servant."

The Bedford Gazette of January 8, 1897, says:

In S. A. Cessna the county has had a trustworthy Treasurer. Of unswerving integrity, alert and accommodating, he has been a safe guardian of the public funds. On February 5th the Gazette further says that Mr. Cessna's accounts were found to be in "apple pie" order, and he again assumes the role of a private citizen conscious of having performed his duties as Treasurer faithfully and well.

The Bedford Inquirer of January 8, 1897, says:

S. A. Cessna, who retired from the office of Treasurer of Bedford County a few days ago, was a successful and accommodating officer. During his term of office he made many friends among the people who had business to transact in his office.

AUTOBIOGRAPHY OF DR. W. R. CISNA

Dr. W. R. Cisna was born in Chambersburg, Pa., December 8, 1837. His father's name was William Cisna, and his mother's maiden name was Everidge, of Norfolk, Va. Of a family of eight children he and his sister, Mrs. Martha Swisher, now living on the Cisna Homestead in Perry County, are the only surviving children of William and Anna Cisna; the others died in infancy. In the year 1845 his parents moved to Cisna Run, the birthplace of his father. Here the subject of this sketch attended the public schools in the winter and in the summer time engaged in farming, and before he was of age, on examination was granted a teacher's certificate and taught in the winter season at Wormley's, Centre and Green Point districts in the county and finally entered Mt. Dempsey Academy in Landisburg, Pa., and there prepared for Dickinson College, at Carlisle, Pa., where he graduated in the year 1863 and received his degree in the college chapel. The public commencement exercises were not held as usual in the City Hall because the Confederate army took possession of Carlisle at that time. This was the only time in the history of Dickinson College, so far as can be learned, that the graduating class had no commencement exercises. The subject of this sketch during the last two years of his college course decided on the study of medicine, and through the counsel of eminent medical men of Carlisle and Perry County prepared to enter the medical department of the University of Pennsylvania, and there received the degree of doctor of medicine in the year 1865, and when a call for surgeons was made at a special examination he was recommended for a vacancy, and was at once ordered to the front and assigned to the forces operating in front of Petersburg and Richmond, Va., and was among the first to enter the city of Richmond on April 3, 1865, and only a few hours after Jefferson Davis left his beautiful mansion. The subject of this sketch also remembers the last time he saw President Lincoln. It was when

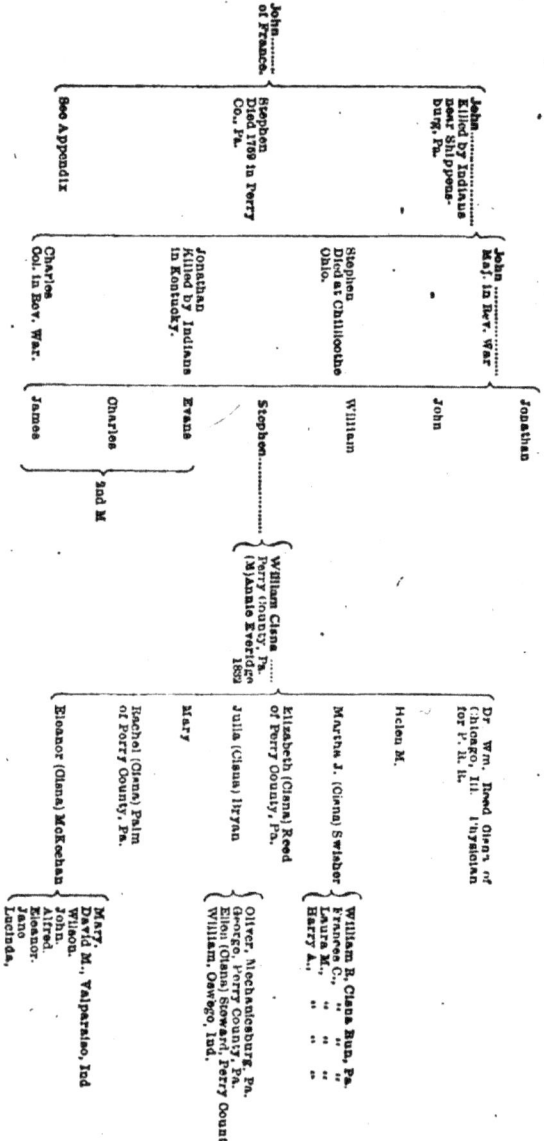

he and a part of his cabinet and several members of his family reviewed the troops then located about seven miles from Richmond, in sight of the pickets of the opposing army in the month of March, 1865, thirty days before his assassination and about two weeks before the army was ordered to move onto Richmond and after remaining a short time in that city he was ordered to Petersburg, Va., to examine recruits for the regular army and says when General Lee surrendered on April 9th of that year the war of 1861 was not entirely over, because General Kirby Smith was contending with our forces in Texas; after the above date several thousand men were ordered to the State named, and in May, at least a month after the surrender of Lee to Grant, the last fight of the war of 1861 occurred on the banks of the Rio Grande river in Texas. He was one of the surgeons sent to Texas for this conflict and while sitting on a camp stool in Virginia received an order to report for duty on a steamer bound for Texas and was made chief medical officer of several batteries of the regular artillery, and finally after a dangerous and tedious voyage disembarked on the coast of Texas and spent almost a year on the frontier. Part of the time he was executive officer in the Post Hospital and had charge of the officers ward, was finally ordered north to be mustered out of the service, and during the administration of President Lincoln was granted a commission of brevet Major for meritorious services in the field. On returning to civil life he located in medical practice in Landisburg, Pa., during which time he traveled over a large territory and was successful in his professional work and to-day has many warm friends in his old field of labor. His many acts of kindness have not been forgotten and his tenderness at the bedside of the afflicted is still fresh in the memory of his old acquaintances. In the year 1876 he married Jennie E. Kiner, they have one son and one daughter. Part of the year his family remains in Ickesburg, Pa., and part of the time in Chicago. His son, Charles, is 21 years of age and his daughter, Helen, is almost 14. In politics he is always reasonable, in religion strictly orthodox;

88

whether people differ from him in his well grounded Republican principles and in church preferences he thinks nothing the less of them for their differences. In the year 1889 Dr. Cisna came to Chicago as medical examiner of the Pennsylvania lines west of Pittsburg, and during his years of service has endeavored to do his duty and has had in his years of service in this line an opportunity of meeting many people in this great city of the west. He has made over 12,000 physical examinations, attended many hundred cases of disablement, has traveled many thousand miles by steam and street cars and has administered to the suffering and sorrowful, has passed through several railroad strikes and has endeavored to preserve harmony among the many employes in his district, and to-day feels highly gratified that he has lived to see success crown his humble efforts, and attributes all to his untiring determination to do his duty, faithful to his employers and impartial to those entrusted to his care. He has never sought political honor and often has politely declined to run in his party ticket but at the solicitation of many of the good citizens of Chicago accepted the appointment of election judge in one of the wards in that city, and received his commission from one of the honorable judges of Cook County. During the years he has noticed the results of the chief executive of the city in both Republican and Democratic rule, and realizing the fact that all the chief executive officials may have been unkindly and unjustly criticised when each may have been trying to do his duty, takes pleasure in stating that he frankly believes the present Mayor is endeavoring to study the best interests of Chicago. He possesses the fine executive qualifications of his father. His decisions are impartial and believes his recommendations are for the good of the citizens, and if he continues in this course of government his good name will be further honored and will be truly classed among the most useful, faithful and honest officials of Chicago.

We thus briefly chronicle the sketch of one of the most worthy sons of Perry County. Having made for himself a splendid record, he has reached the zenith of his usefulness

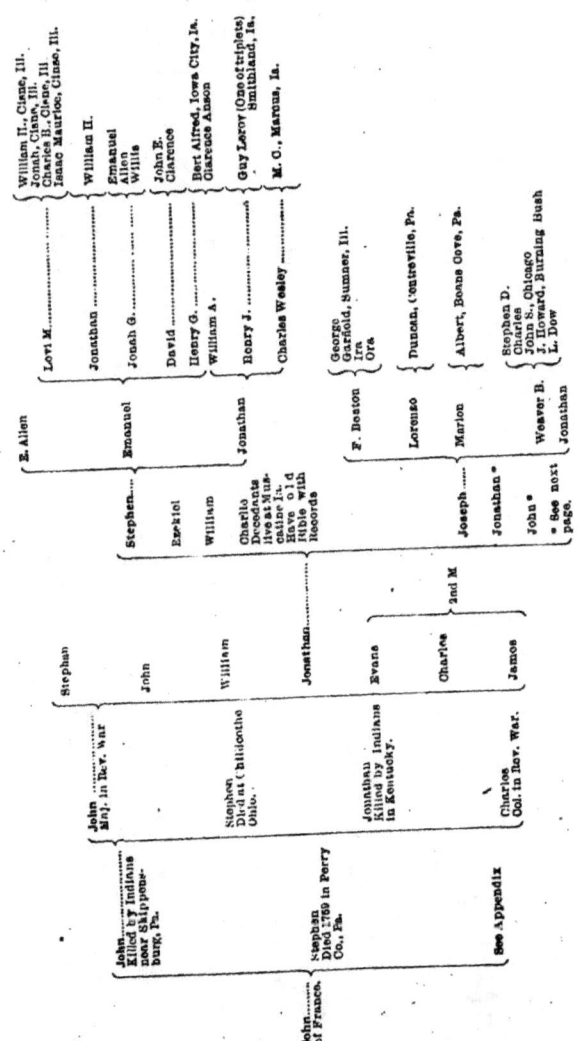

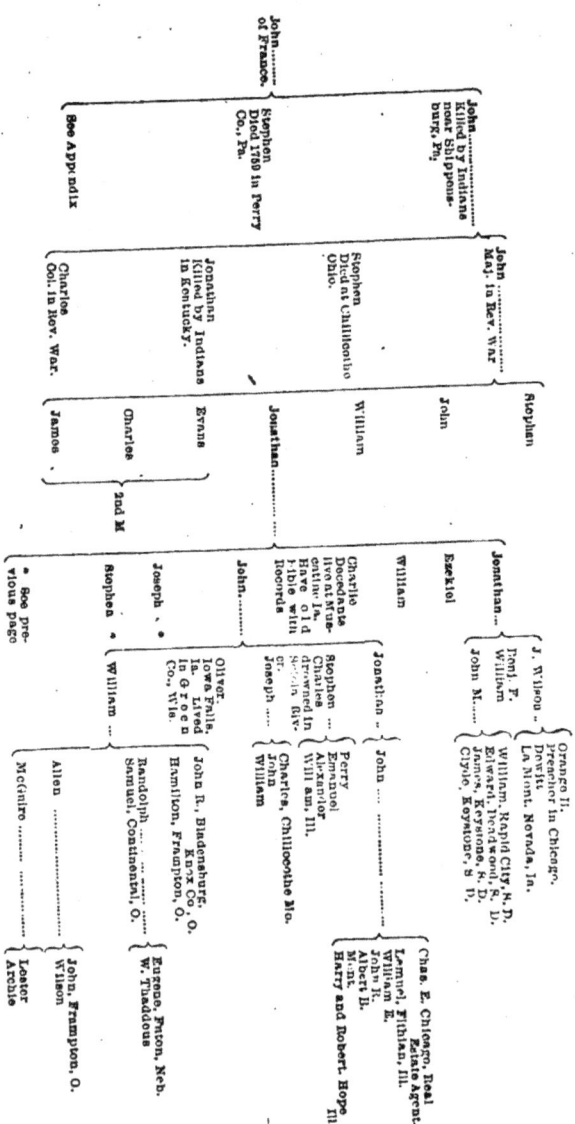

91

ranking now with the leading physicians and surgeons of Chicago. The writer has a pardonable pride in sending this communication for publication from the fact that within a mile from Cisna Run he first saw the light and can remember the horizon of his boyhood was limited by the mountains and hills encircling that lovely spot in Perry, and among the families well remembered as we revert in thought to those days, is the one mentioned in this sketch of which Dr. W. R. Cisna is an honored son.

Published by Rev. J. Dill Calhoun, of Knoxville, Ill.

Jonathan Cessna IV,
John III, John II, John I.

Was born November 16, 1760, died February 14, 1853, age, 92. Married Rebecca Worley, who was born August 16, 1764, and died July 29, 1815. Issue: (1) John, born August 26, 1780, died April 23, 1832. (2) Stephen, born April 17, 1782, died June 3, 1829. (3) Charles, born February 7, 1874. (4) Sarah, born November 18, 1786, died April 13, 1844. (5) Jonathan, born April 1, 1789. (6) Ezekiel, born May 12, 1791. (7) Margaret, born December 23, 1792. (8) Rachel, born June 1, 1795. (9) William, born December 21, 1797, died February 3, 1843. (10) Joseph, born October 29, 1801, died November 4, 1854. (11) Rebecca, born March 5, 1804. (12) Elenor, born November 16, 1807, died November 11, 1852.

JONATHAN CESSNA V, JONATHAN, IV.

Died October 17, 1868, age, 72. Married Catharine Boor September 14, 1820, who was born in 1801 and died

June 7, 1870. Issue: (1) Helen, born November 13, 1821.
(2) Louisa, born March 5, 1823. (3) J. Wilson, born
October 27, 1824. (4) Benjamin F., born January 27, 1826.
(5) Perry, born December 29, 1827. (6) Caroline, born
November 30, 1829. (7) Virginia, born February 12, 1832.
(8) William, born August 7, 1836. (9) Harriet, born September 9, 1838. (10) John, born August 26, 1844.

J. WILSON CESSNA VI, Jonathan v.

Address, Nevada, Iowa. Occupation, retired farmer.
Married May 8, 1851, Elizabeth Jane Matthews, born April
7, 1834. Issue: (1) Orange H., born July 31, 1852. (2)
Dewitt, born August 5, 1854. (3) May, born January 1,
1858. (4) La Mont, born February 22, 1860. (5) Zella, (6)
Wilda, (7) Ginevera.

ORANGE H. CESSNA, (VII), J. Wilson, (VI).

Occupation, minister. Address, Chicago, Ill. Married
Lilliam May Wheeler, of Chicago, Ill., August 31, 1881.
Issue: (1) Ethel, born June 4, 1884. (2) Frank W., born
December 1, 1885.

DEWITT CESSNA, (VII), J. Wilson, (VI).

Died January 30, 1870.

MAY CESSNA, (VII), J. Wilson, (VI).

Died August 27, 1859.

LA MONT CESSNA, (VII), J. Wilson, (VI).

Address, Nevada, Iowa. Occupation, farmer. Married
Minnie Bechtel. Issue: (1) Ruth, (2) Hazel, (3) Karl.

JONATHAN WILSON CESSNA.
Page 62.

ZELLA CESSNA, (VII), J. Wilson, (VI).

Address, Ottumwa, Iowa. Married January 20, 1886, Jonathan H. Fitton, a contractor and collector for McCormick Harvester Machine Company. No issue.

WILDA CESSNA, (VII), J. Wilson, (VI).

Address, Ottumwa, Iowa. Married November 6, 1889, John W. Neasham, who came from Easby, Yorkshire, England, in 1881, and at present conducts one of the largest jewelry establishments in Southern Iowa. Issue: (1) Donald Joseph, born July 4, 1895. (2) Elizabeth and Margaret, twins, born September 4, 1897.

GINEVERA CESSNA, (VII), J. Wilson, (VI).

Address, Nevada, Iowa. Occupation, teacher. Single.

HELEN CESSNA VI, Jonathan V, Jonathan IV, John III.

Married William Dougherty. Issue: (1) Frank Cessna Dougherty, (2) J. Wallace, (3) Howard, (4) May. Two of these boys are lawyers in Kenton, Ohio.

LOUISA CESSNA VI.

Married Anthony Banning. Issue: (1) Jonathan Cessna, a physician; (2) Nancy, (3) Kate, (4) Sophia, (5) Caroline, (6) Amos, (7) Helen. Address, Kenton, Ohio.

CAROLINE CESSNA VI,

Married D. N. Foreman. Address, Los Angeles, Cal.

PERRY CESSNA VI, Jonathan V.

Lived in Arkansas. Had three sons.

HARRIET EVE CESSNA VI.

Married Ira M. Moore. Issue: (1) Shelby Cessna, a teacher; (2) Hurbert M.

CHARLES CESSNA VL.

Married Ann ———, of Cumberland Valley, Pa. Issue: (1) James, (2) Rachel Rebecca, (3) Mary C., (4) Charles William, (5), Emeline. Descendants live in Whiteside County, Illinois.

JOHN MARTIN CESSNA VI, Jonathan V, Jonathan iv.

Born August 26, 1844, died October 11, 1884. Married Adelaide Rogers November 15, 1865. Issue: (1) Nancy, (2) Emma, (3) Willia., (4) Edward, (5) James, (6) Clyde.

NANCY CESSNA, (VII), John Martin, (VI).

Born August 18, 1866. Address, Keystone, S. D. Married William Rice. Issue: (1) John, (2) Pauline, (3) William, (4) Reginald.

EMMA CESSNA, (VII), John Martin, (VI).

Born May 2, 1868. Address, Rapid City, S. D. Married, James Barber, postmaster of Rapid City. Issue: (1) Gerald, (2) Paul, (3) Howard.

WILLIAM CESSNA, (VII), John Martin, (VI).

Born June 9, 1870. Address, Rapid City, S. D.

EDWARD CESSNA, (VII), John Martin, (VI).

Born February 16, 1872. Address, Deadwood, S. D.

COL. WILLIAM T. CESSNA.
Pages 78 and 62.

97

JAMES CESSNA, (VII), John Martin, (VI).

Born May 2, 1879. Address, Keystone, S. D.

CLYDE CESSNA, (VII), John Martin, (VI).

Born September 17, 1884. Address, Keystone, S. D.

JOSEPH CESSNA V, JONATHAN IV.

Born October 29, 1801. Married Ann Barnes, of Maryland, a daughter of Major Barnes who served in the Revolutionary War with General Washington. Issue: (1) Jonathan, born January 21, 1824, and married Susan Martin. (2) Harriet, born November 28, 1825. (3) Lorenzo, born October 6, 1827, married Hannah Henderson. (4) Savilla, born December 21, 1829, married Jonathan Hendrickson. (5) Weaver B. Cessna, born March 17, 1832. (6) Eliza, born 1834, died before she was one year old. (7) Marion, born November 12, 1835, married Susan Hardman. (8) Louisa, born January 19, 1838, married John A. Wertz, of Bedford, Pa. (9) T. Benton, born September 27, 1840, married to Mary Martin, of Illinois.

T. BENTON CESSNA VI, Joseph V, Jonathan iv.

Born September 27, 1840, died February 19, 1890, in Illinois. Married Susan Martin. Issue: (1) Lilly, (2) Myrtle, (3) George, (4) Garfield, (5) Ira, (6) Oro.

LILLY CESSNA, (VII), T. Benton, (VI).

Born July 26, 1875. Address, Birds, Ill. Married T. H. Pinkstaff, a farmer. Issue: Lyman.

Myrtle Cessna, (VII,) T. Benton, (VI). Address, Olney, Ill.

Ora Cessna, (VII), T. Benton, (VI). Address Huntingdon, Ind..

98

George Cessna, (VII), T. Benton, (VI). Address Sumner, Ill.

Garfield Cessna, (VII), T. Benton, (VI). Address, Sumner, Ill.

Ira Cessna, (VII), T. Benton, (VI). Address, Bedford, Pa.

LORENZO CESSNA VI, Joseph V, Jonathan iv, John III.

Born 1827, died 1898. Married Hannah Hendrickson. Occupation, farmer and stockman. Was a great fiddler. Issue: (1) Alice, (2) Duncan, (3) Louisa.

ALICE CESSNA, (VII) Lorenzo, (VI), Joseph, (V).

Address, Lafayette County, Missouri. Married Forrest Snowden. Issue: (1) Glen, (2) Pearl.

LOUISA CESSNA, (VII), Lorenzo, (VI).

Died at Cumberland, Md. Married George Hite. Issue: (1) Walter, who married Gertrude Cessna, of Rainsburg, Pa., and lives near Centreville, Pa.

DUNCAN CESSNA, (VII), Lozenzo, (VI).

Address, Centreville, Pa. Married Annie Hite. Issue: (1) Barney, born February 2, 1888. (2) Charlotte, (3) Marion. Duncan Cessna is a farmer and like his father a fiddler and banjo player.

MARION CESSNA VI. Joseph V, Jonathan iv, John iii.

Married Susan Hardman. Lived at Sumner, Ill., and died there. Issue: (1) Blanche, (2) Buella, (3) Albert.

BLANCHE CESSNA AND BUELA CESSNA, (VII), Marion, (VI).

Married Ambrose Cessna. Issue:

ALBERT CESSNA, (VII), Marion, (VI).

Married Mollie Summerville. Issue: (1) Carl, (2) Lina. Address, Bean's Cove, Pa.

WEAVER B. CESSNA VI, Joseph V, Jonathan iv, Joon iii.

Born March 17, 1832. Married Ann Snowden, February 25, 1853. Address, Burning Bush, Pa. Farmer and a great fiddler. Issue: (1) Francis Eugenia, born November 24, 1855. (2) Eldesta Idella, born July 31, 1857. (3) Florence Evelyn, born November 29, 1858. (4) Stephen D., born August 24, 1860. (5) Charles C., born January 25, 1863. (6) John S., born February 4, 1865. (7) Mary Rosmond, born October 11, 1866. (8) Joseph Howard, born August 19, 1868. (9) Clara Violet, born May 31, 1870. (10) Anna Myrtle, born August 5, 1872. (1) Ethel Grame, born February 28, 1875. (12) Glendora, born February 23, 1878. (13) Louisa, born August 15, ~~1882.~~ *1883* (14) Lorenzo Dow, born August 2, ~~1884.~~ *1885*

FRANCES EUGENIA CESSNA, (VII), Weaver B., (VI).

Address, Newton, Kansas. Married J. F. Carpenter, a merchant. Issue: (1) Ola, (2) Walter, (3) Evelyn, (4) Oscar, (5) Nellie, (6) Allen.

ELDESTA IDELLA CESSNA, (VII), Weaver B., (VI).

Address, Fostoria, Ohio. Married J. S. Wertz, a landlord. Issue: (1) Sherman, (2) Mary, (3) Annie, (4) John, (5) Grover, (6) Samuel.

FLORENCE EVELYN CESSNA, (VII), Weaver B., (VI).

Address, Chicago, Ill. Married N. S. Brubaker, an employe of Chicago Steel Mills. Issue: (1) Pearl, (2) Flossie.

STEPHEN DOUGLASS CESSNA (VII), Weaver B. (VI).

Address, Pittsburg, Pa. Occupation, carpenter. Married (1) Bridget O'Shea. Issue: (1) Percy, (2) Bertha, (3) Elsie. Married (2) Miss Weichman.

CHARLES CARROLL CESSNA, (VII), Weaver B., (VI).

Address, Bedford, Pa. Married Mary Beemiller. Issue: Norman, et. al.

JOHN SNOWDEN CESSNA, (VII), Weaver B., (VI).

Address, Chicago, Ill. Occupation, operator. He was in the Spanish War and wrote a letter home which was printed in the Bedford Gazette in 1898.

MARY ROSAMOND CESSNA, (VII), Weaver B., (VI).

Address, Yellow Creek, Pa. Married Phil. A. Barnett, a bottler. Issue: (1) Eugene, born February 5, 1899.

ANNA MYRTLE CESSNA, (VII), Weaver B., (VI).

Address, Blain, Perry County, Pa. Married Dr. H. O. Lightner October 13, 1896. Issue: (1) Linn.

ETHEL GRAME CESSNA, (VII), Weaver B., (VI).

Address, Pittsburg, Pa. Single. Stenographer for Attorney Negley.

GLENDORA CESSNA, (VII), Weaver B., (VI).

Address, Pittsburg, Pa. Single. Stenographer.

LEVI M. CISNE.
Pp. 69 and 79.

102

LOUISA CESSNA, (VII), Weaver B., (VI).

Address, Saxton, Pa. Single. Student.

LORENZO DOW CESSNA, (VII), Weaver B., (VI).

Address, Burning Bush, Pa. Single.

STEPHEN CESSNA V, JONATHAN IV.

Born April 17, 1782, died June 2, 1829. Occupation, miller and sickle maker. Changed spelling of his name to Cisne so that name could be painted on sickle. Married Mary Rose, who was born March 3, 1787. Issue: (1) Stephen, born November 18, 1811. (2) Jonathan, born May 19, 1815. (3) Elenor, born May 27, 1818. (4) Agnes, born September 13, 1821. (5) Sarah, born March 19, 1824. (6) Ezekiel Allen, born April 17, 1826. (7) Margaret Ann, born September 20, 1829. (8) Emanuel.

EMANUEL CESSNA -- CISNE -- VI, Stephen V.

Born February 4, 1807, died June 4, 1879. Occupation, farmer, teacher and Brigadier General of Ohio Militia. Married Sarah Girard of the family of Girards of Pennsylvania. Issue: (1) Levi M., (2) Jonathan, (3) Jonah G., (4) Mary E., (5) David A., (6), Nancy J., (7) Henry G., (8) Eunice A., (9) Sarah C.

LEVI M. CESSNA (CISNE), (VII), Emanuel, (VI).

Born December 28, 1830, died in 1892 at Cisne, Ill. Married Jane Ray. Issue: (1) William H., (2) Mary C., (3) Sarah J., (4) Jonah, (5) Julia Ann, (6) Agnes, (7) Charles B., (8) Edna Pearl, (9) Isaac Maurice.

JONATHAN CESSNA (CISNE), (VII), Emanuel, (VI).

Born July 29, 1832, died in the winter of 1866. Married Sarah Bollinger. Issue: (1) Ella, (2) Mary, (3) William H.

JONATHAN CISNE

Jonathan Cisne, a son of Emanuel Cisne, was born in Monroe County, Ohio, July 28, 1832. He received a fair education and at an early age was employed on a steamboat plying between Cincinnati and New Orleans. He came to Illinois in the year 18— and went into the mercantile business at Flora, Ill. He was married to Sarah Bolinger in the year 1857 at Flora, Clay County, Ill. He went to Pikes Peak prospecting. In 1860 he came home, returning to the Rocky Mountains in 1861. He came home again in the winter of 1861 and volunteered in the war of 1862. He was retained in service as Provost-Marshal at Columbus, Ky., serving until the following Spring. He was then detailed as a Government Detective, serving as such until May 28, 1865, being discharged at Trenton, N. J. He died seven months after arriving home on January 16, 1865, being 33 years of age.

[Written by W. H. Cisne, "Jun," only son of Jonathan Cisne, Zenith, Ill.]

JONAH G. CESSNA (CISNE), (VII), Emanuel, (VI).

Born August 25, 1834, died in 1877. Married Sevilla Towns. Issue: (1) Emanuel, (2) Lorema, (3) Allen, (4) Willis, (5) Vergie.

MARY E. CESSNA (CISNE), (VII), Emanuel, (VI).

Born April 24, 1836, died November 23, 1889. Married Ezra Phillips. Issue: (1) Margaret, (2) Charles N., (3) Sarah J., (4) Elmer, (5) William, (6) Mary E., (7) Fred, (8) Eva Kate, (9) Eddy.

DAVID A. CESSNA (CISNE), (VII), Emanuel, (VI).

Address Cisne, Ill. Born December 25, 1837. Occupation, farmer. Married (1) Anna Cory. Issue: (1) Sarah

W. H. CISNE.
Pages 69 and 70.

105

THE HOUSE OF CESSNA.

L., (2) Louis May, (3) Minnie, (4) John E, (5) Artelia. Married (2) Lizzie Schofield. Issue: (1) Clarence.

NANCY CESSNA (CISNE), (VII), Emanuel, (VI).

Born December 9, 1840, died in the winter of 1886. Married George H. Crawford, of Antioch, Ohio. Issue: (1) Oliver, (2) Luretta, (3) Robert E., (4) S rah, (5) Luna Dell, (6) William.

EUNICE ANN CESSNA (CISNE), (VII), Emanuel, (VI).

Born September 26, 1845, died April 23, 1894. Married F. M. Amos. Issue: (1) James O., (2) Henry O., (3) Robert, (4) Corben, (5) Earnest, (6) Jessie, (7) Francis Marion, (8) Eunice Ann, (9) Walter Scott, (10) Knox.

SARAH C. (KATE CISNE). CESSNA, (VII), Emanuel, (VI).

Born October 29, 1849. Address Fairfield, Wayne County, Ill. Married James P. Walters, a physician and surgeon. Issue: (1) DeForest E., (2) Luna Dell, (3) Freddie Earl, (4) Charles Eddy, (5) Elmer Kramer, (6) Anna Lee.

JONATHAN CISNE VI, Stephen v, Jonathan iv,

Married Julia Ann Wink. Issue: (1) Christiana J., born in Monroe County, Ohio, March 18, 1840. (2) Stephen B., born in Monroe County, Ohio, August 28, 1841. (3) William, born in Monroe County, Ohio, February 7, 1843. (4) Jonathan (Iowa City) born July 7, 1845. (5) Hannah, born in Newport, Iowa, November 27, 1847. (6) Lewis, born October 27, 1849. (7) Henry, born November 17, 1851. (8) John W., born October 17, 1853. (9) Mary A., born August 22, 1855. (10) George W., born April 18, 1857. (11) Charles W., born October 27, 1859. (12) William A., born May 20, 1861.

The addresses of the above are as follows: Christiana,

Fort Dodge, Iowa, family; Henry, Smithland, Iowa, family; Charles, Marcus, Iowa, family; George, Council Bluffs, Iowa, family; Mary Eichorn, Walnut Grove, Iowa, family; Hannah Allbright, Hanson, Neb., family; W. A., Iowa City.

WILLIAM A. CISNE, (VII), Jonathan, (VI), Stephen, (V).

Address, Iowa City, Iowa. Born in Johnson County, Iowa, May 20, 1861. Married Emma Hoffman . Issue: (1) Bert Alfred, born April 29, 1884. (2) Clarence Anson, born June 6, 1894. (3) Mabel, born January 15, 1896.

HANNAH CISNE, (VII).

Address, Hanson, Neb. Born November 22, 1847. Married F. Allbright. Issue: (1) Emma E., born May 12, 1867. (2) Julia Ann, born February 22, 1869. (3) William Nelson, born April 6, 1870. (4) Adaline E., born February 6, 1872. (5) August Frederick, born September 29, 1875, at West Blue, Neb. (6) Mary Louisa, born January 23, 1878. (7) Clara Bell, born July 1, 1870. (8) M. Amelia, born November 28, 1882. (9) Hannah M., born December 31, 1884. (10) Carrie May, born September 18, 1886. (11) Nellie C., born July 16, 1891.

HENRY J. CISNE, (VII).

Address, Smithland, Iowa. Born in Johnson County, Iowa, November 17, 1851. Married Sarad M. Craft. Issue: (1) Grace Maude, (2) Elsie May, (3-4-5) Bessie, Daisy and Guy Leroy, triplets, born January 31, 1892. (6) Hazel, born February 23, 1893. (7) Myrtle, born November 5, 1894. (8) Cressie L., born November 7, 1897.

CHARLES WESLEY CISNE, (VII).

Address, Marcus, Iowa. Born at Newport, Iowa, October 12, 1857. Married Mary Louise Weber, of Newark, N. J. Issue: (1) M. C., born September 17, 1884. (2) Bessie Mable, born February 20, 1888. (3) J. Florence, born September 13, 1891.

MARY CISNE, (VII).

Address, Walnut, Iowa. Born August 22, 1855. Married Edward Eichorn, of Philadelphia, Pa. Issue: (1) Charles Raymond, born April 8, 1882. (2) Alma Grace, born April 2, 1890. (3) Earl Edwin, born October 3, 1892. (4) Mable L., born July 18, 1896.

JOHN CESSNA V, JONATHAN IV.

Married Mary McVicker. Went to Ohio about 1822; settled in Pike Township, Coshocton County. Issue: (1) Nancy, (2) Jonathan, (3) Rebecca, (4) Stephen, (5) Charles, (6) Rachel, (7) Elizabeth, (8) John, (9) Mary, (10) Joseph, (11) Maria, a twin with Joseph, (12) William, (13) Oliver, (14) Hannah.

NANCY CESSNA VI, John v.

Married William Lemert. Issue: (1) John C., (2) Mary, (3) Eliza, (4) Charles, (5) William, (6) Hannah, (7) Louis, (8) Minerva.

JONATHAN CESSNA VI, John v.

Married Margaret Divan. Issue: (1) John, (2) Elizabeth.

REBECCA CESSNA VI, John v.

Married Lloyd Lemert. Issue: Ten children. They live in Marshall County, near Plymouth, Indiana.

STEPHEN CESSNA VI, John v.

Married Elizabeth Lemert. Issue: (1) Perry, (2)

Emanuel, (3) Alexandria, (4) William, who is the only one living. He lives somewhere in Illinois.

CHARLES CESSNA VI, John v.

Married a woman from Franklin County, Ohio. Her maiden name not secured. Both were drowned a few days after their marriage in the Sciota River.

RACHEL CESSNA VI, John v.

Married John Shrake. Issue: Eight children, names unknown to author. They live somewhere in Wisconsin.

ELIZABETH CESSNA VI, John v.

Died unmarried at the age of 18.

JOHN CESSNA VI, John v.

Died unmarried at the age of 23.

MARY CESSNA VI, John v.

Married John Wright. Issue: (1) Olive, (2) Elizabeth, (3) Delilah, (4) William, (5) Edward, (6) Mary, (7) David, (8) Hannah, (9) Ellen, (10) Sarah, (11) Nancy.

JOSEPH CESSNA VI, John v.

Married Nancy Mercer. Issue: (1) Charles, (2) Lucinda, (3) Mary, (4) John, (5) William. Charles post office address is Chillicothe, Missouri.

MARIAH CESSNA VI, John v.

Died when an infant. She was a twin of Joseph.

OLIVER CESSNA VI, John v

Address, Iowa Falls, Marshall County, Iowa. Married a Miss Baughman. Moved from Ohio in 1845 to Wisconsin, in Greene County. Names of children unknown to author.

HANNAH CESSNA VI, John v

Married Frederick Divan. Issue: Nine children. They live near Seward, Seward County, Nebraska.

WILLIAM CESSNA VI, John v

Married (1) Elizabeth Rine in 1842. *25 Aug* Issue: (1) John R., born June 9, 1844. (2) Hamilton, born April 6, 1846. (3) Rudolph, born November 26, 1848. (4) Eliza Ellen, born December 2, 1850. William Thaddeus, born December 22, 1853. Married (2) Margaret M. Rine, 1861. Issue: (1) Samuel, (2) Allen, (3) McGuire.

HAMILTON, (VII), William, (VI), John, (V).

Address, Frampton, Licking County, Ohio. Widower. No issue.

JOHN R. CESSNA, (VII), William, (VI), John, (V).

Address, Bladensburg, Knox County, Ohio. Occupation, stockdealer and Justice of the Peace. Married February 17, 1874, Sarah Norris, of Coshocton County, Ohio. No Issue.

RUDOLPH CESSNA, (VII), William, (VI), John, (V).

Address, Fulton, Seward County, Nebraska. Married Nancy Williams, of Green County, Wisconsin. Issue: (1) Eugene, (2) Wright, (3) Earnest, (4) Eva, (5) Minnie, (6) Wilber, (7) George, (8) Spencer, (9) Mary, (10) Alice.

110

ELIZA E. CESSNA, (VII), William, (VI), John, (V).

Married William Murray. Address, Lacona, Iowa. Issue: Charles.

WILLIAM THADDEUS, (VII), William, (VI), John, (V).

Married Nancy Baird. Issue: (1) Viola, (2) Iva, (3) Daisy.

SAMUEL CESSNA, (VII), William, (VI), John, (V).

Born February 23, 1862. Address, Continental, Putnam County, Ohio. Married Lavina Farquar. Issue: (1) Arla, (2) Etha.

ALLEN CESSNA, (VII), William, (VI), John, (V).

Born January 19, 1864. Address, Frampton, Licking County, Ohio. Married Vesta Wilson. Issue: (1) Maggie, (2) Eula, (3) Stella, (4) John, (5) Wilson.

McGUIRE CESSNA, (VII), William, (VI), John, (V).

Born September 28, 1865. Address, Frampton, Licking County, Ohio. Married Lizzie McQuee. Issue: (1) Rosella, (2) Mary, (3) Lester Archie.

JOHN CESSNA, (VII), Jonathan, (VI), John, (V), Jonathan, (IV).

Address, Hope, Ill. Occupation, farmer. Born June 29, 1833. Married (1) Ann R. Truax. Issue: (1) Charles E. Cessna, Real Estate Agent, 1582 Mozart Street, Chicago, Ill. (2) Lemuel E., address, Fithian, Ill. (3) Elizabeth, Stenographer. (4) William E., (5) Mary A. Married (2) Nancy J. Read. Issue: (1) Anna R., (2) John R., (3) Albert B., (4) Mont P., (5) Harry F., (6) Hester, (7) Robert, (8) Nancy A.

REV. O. H. CESSNA.
Page 77.

112

SARAH CESSNA V, Jonathan IV.

Married Mr. Stephens and moved to Shawken County, Ohio.

RACHEL CESSNA V.

Married Mr. Hemming, Cumberland Valley, Pa. Issue: Margaret, intermarried with Sam Elliott; Rebecca, intermarried with Alex. Rose, of Indiana; H. W. Hemming; Sisen, married Mr. McFerrin. Cumberland Valley, Pa.; Matilda, married Mr. Bennett, of Hyndman, Pa.; Liza, married Mr. Defibaugh, of Hebron, W. Va.; Nansa. Harden County, Ohio; Joseph; Richard; Julia, married Mr. Norris, Cumberland Valley, Pa.

REBECCA CESSNA V, JONATHAN IV.

Married Mr. Hemming. Issue: George, Carle County, Ohio; John; Henry, Johnson County, Indiana; Charles, Fostoria, Ohio; Matilda, married Mr. Rouse; Rachel, married Mr. Dunlap. Canton, Ohio; Margaret, married Mr. Haney, Canton, Ohio.

REV. O. H. CESSNA , D. D.

Rev. O. H. Cessna, D. D., pastor of Wesley Church, Chicago, has been unanimously elected professor of history and ethics in the Iowa State College of Agriculture and Mechanic Arts at Ames, Iowa, and has accepted. The institution had about 1,000 students enrolled the past year. Dr. Cessna is an alumnus of the college, having graduated in its first class in '72. He entered Northwestern University, where he pursued a classical course and graduated from Garrett Biblical Institute with B. D. in '85. He has specialized in history and ethics and received the degree of D. D. from Garrett at its recent commencement. Dr. Cessna joined the Rock River conference in 1885, and has been pastor at Belvidere; First church. Elgin; Dixon and

113

Wesley Church, Chicago. He will continue his membership in Rock River conference. The Iowa State College is one of the best equipped institutions of its kind in the United States. Hon. James Wilson, Secretary of Agriculture, is a member of its faculty, on leave of absence.

DR. B. F. CESSNA

[Written by J. Wilson Cessna, of Nevada, Iowa.]

Dr. B. F. Cessna was born in Cumberland Valley, Bedford County, Pa., January 26, 1826, and came, with his parents, to Coshocton County, Ohio, in the Spring of 1826, where they lived until the Spring of 1833. They then moved to Hardin County, Ohio, where he grew to manhood attending school in Winter and working on his father's farm in Summer. He then went to the Ohio Weslyan University, at Delaware, Ohio, and graduated. Coming home he studied both branches of the medical profession in Kenton and practiced there a short time. He then attended the medical college at Ann Arbor, Michigan, and graduated. He then married and practiced his profession until 1857 when he attended Jefferson Medical College, Philadelphia. He then came back to Ohio and practiced his profession and made a large fortune. He gave $30,000 to the Ohio Wesleyan University to establish a B. F. Cessna professorship. He now lives in Kenton, Ohio.

COL. WILLIAM T. CESSNA

Col. William T. Cessna was born in Hardin County, Ohio, in 1836, and lived at home attending school in Winter and working on the farm in Summer until of age when he attended the N. W. University, at Delaware, Ohio, and graduated, came home and studied law in Kenton, was admitted to the bar, and at the breaking out of the war of the rebellion was appointed First Lieutenant and was with General Pope in his Virginia campaign. He was promoted to captain and finally colonel, and at the close of the war was elected to represent Hardin County in the Legislature by

DR. B. F. CESSNA.
Page 78.

PROF. WILLIS GIRARD CISNE.
Page 79.

116

the Democratic party. He was married, but had no children. He was a member and secretary of a company that laid out a suburb of Chicago. He afterward became president of a large mining company of Cripple Creek, Colorado, and has since been traveling in Europe.

PROF. WILLIS GIRARD CISNE

W. G. Cisne, son of J. G. Cisne, born near Cisne, Ill., February 13, 1875. Attended the district school until 18 years of age and then received license to teach. Taught one year in Wayne and two years in Logan County. Entered the State Normal University at Carbondale in September, 1896, and graduated in the English course in June, 1899, since which time he has been connected with the public schools of Fairfield, Ill. At present is Principal of the High School.

ADDRESS DELIVERED AT FAMILY REUNION, FAIRFIELD, ILL.

Again there is an occasion to report a day well and happily spent. Three families—The Cisne, Ray and Stine—were represented. The guests had been invited to meet at the home of Mrs. Jane Cisne, widow of the late Levi M. Cisne. Children, grandchildren and great grandchildren, brothers, sisters, aunts, uncles, grandfathers, grandmothers, and relatives of every description were there.

The morning looked quite stormy, preventing some from coming, but by noon the clouds had cleared away. Soon we were on our way to the beautiful park, which is but a short distance from the house, and which had been chosen and named for our brave Sampson. Comfortable seats had been erected. Table spread that was almost unable to bear its weight. Stumps were designated for the speakers. All things were ready, and soon the register counted the number 96.

After dinner (which was not only bountiful but delicious), Dr. J. P. Walters took a stump, giving, as introductory remarks, the cause for this gathering of people. A sister of Mrs. Jane Cisne, Mrs. Mary Stine (nee Ray), is here from Henrietta, Texas. Also Mrs. Cisne's daughter and son-in-law, Mrs. Julia and Mr. Will Brach, of Chicago. For these she had given the other relatives an invitation to spend the day at her home. He then introduced Mr. Stephen Stine, the oldest of the crowd, an octogenarian, to give a talk concerning the three families.

Mr. Stine gave quite an interesting history of them, in which he proved to us that he has yet a splendid memory. Also that he is quite an orator. Mr. Stine said: "Nearly a century a go a man by the name of Stephen Cisne emigrated from Pennsylvania to Monroe county, Ohio, then an almost unbroken wilderness. He settled on Sunfish Creek. He owned a mill, but was by trade a sickle maker. I have been to his mill very

117

often, and have worn out two of his sickles or reap-hooks. The family formerly spelled the name Cessna, but as Stephen put his name on his sickles, the name was abridged by him to Cisne, and is so retained by the family to this day. I hold in my hand a sword that belonged to one of his sons, Gen. Emanuel Cisne, the father of the Cisnes that came to this county years ago, the oldest of whom was Levi M. Cisne, the husband of our venerable hostess to-day—Mrs. Jane Cisne. Gen. E. Cisne, as we always called him, was one of the finest men I ever knew. One of God's noblemen. He was a military man, and was commissioned Brigadier General of Ohio Militia by Gov. Corwin, which commission is now in the possession of his youngest daughter, Mrs. Dr. J. P. Walters. I used to muster every year under Gen. Cisne's commands as he gave them with this sword, with which we all became familiar. I have in my possession a certificate of disability from him, exempting me from military duty. The General was a prominent man in Monroe county, Ohio. He was elected to county, town and township offices, and always filled some position of trust as long as he lived. When the Civil War broke out he was active in the service of his country, and, although quite old (53 years), he assisted in raising three companies, and drilled them for the front. Went with one of them, and served as military officer for nearly two years. Gen. Cisne married Sarah Girard, of the family of Girards of Pennsylvania fame. Of the Cisnes here I will say nothing, as you all know them as well as I do. Our hostess, Mrs. Jane Cisne, is a daughter of Major Ray. Major Ray was a 'school master' in his day. A gentleman in every sense of the word, and was often called upon by the people to fill some position of trust, which he always did with credit to himself. He came to this country from Monroe county, Ohio, before any of the Cisnes came. The fact is, Levi Cisne followed Major Ray here, because he had a sweetheart in Major Ray's family. Over one hundred years ago a German by the name of Stine came from Fatherland, across the Atlantic to America, and settled at Philadelphia. He raised a large family, and with them emigrated west. One of his sons, Michael, was my father, who married the daughter of a revolutionary soldier by the name of Alton. All went to Western Pennsylvania, in the early day, where it became necessary, at times, to fight Indians. My grandfather Alton had a hand-to-hand conflict with one, and after a struggle, killed him. Michael Stine moved west from Pennsylvania to Monroe county, Ohio, in an early day. He raised a large family, and four of his boys, Eri, Isaac, Peter, and myself, came to this country nearly a half century ago. Of our families you all know the history. All my father's family are laid away in different cemeteries over this great country except your humble speaker. I am ready, and expect to follow them soon. Thanks to you for this occasion and your attention."

In addition to what has been given in the history of the Cisnes I will add a few items: The first Cessna (as it was then spelled) to come to America, was John Cessna, a French Huguenot, who came over in 1690, and settled in Eastern Pennsylvania. He raised a family. Among them was a son, John, who settled near Shippensburg, Pa. Little is known of his family save his son, Major John Cessna, who came to Rainsburg, Bedford county, Pa., in 1765; was a member of the Constitutional Convention of 1776, over which Benjamin Franklin presided; was Sheriff of Bedford county in 1778, and again in 1781. He had a brother who was Colonel in the Revolutionary War. An effort is being made by one of his descendants (Howard Cessna, attorney at law, of Bedford, Pa.), to publish a family genealogy. Also, to erect a granite stone to the memory of Major John Cessna. A circular letter has been received lately by the Cisnes here in reference to this effort.—From an article published in a Fairfield, Ill., paper.

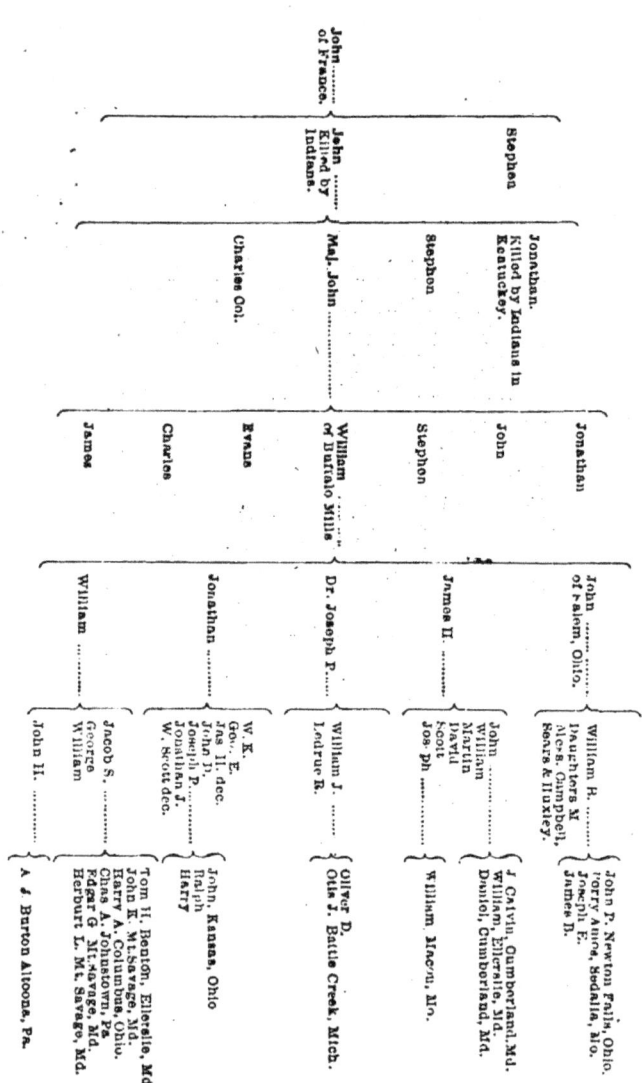

JOHN CESSNA.
Pages 81 and 84.

William Cessna IV,
John III, John II, John I,

Married Nancy E. Barnes, a daughter of Major Barnes, of Maryland. Issue: (1) Mary, (2) John, (3) Sarah, (4) Margaret, (5) James, (6) Jonathan, (7) Rachel, (8) Elizabeth, (9) Joseph.

MARY CESSNA V, WILLLIAM IV.

Married Valentine Lybarger, of Seneca County, Ohio. Died in 1850.

JOHN CESSNA V, WILLIAM IV.

Born September 3, 1803, died June 20, 1890. Was a stockdealer and farmer near Salem, Ohio. Married Jane Cook, of Greene, Mahoning County, Ohio, March 16, 1830, who died February 28, 1893. Issue: (1) Elizabeth Ann, (2) Rachel G., (3) Almira, (4) Mary Jane, (5) Evaline, (6) Maria, (7) Julia, (8) William B.

ELIZABETH ANN CESSNA VI, John V, William iv.

Born December 20, 1830, died February 26, 1852. Married John Campbell, of Salem, Ohio, January 1, 1851. Issue: Charles Cessna Campbell.

CHARLES CESSNA CAMPBELL, (VII), Elizabeth Ann, (VI).

Born February 19, 1852. Occupation, merchant. Ad-

121

dress, Salem, Ohio. Married Florine Grinns November 26, 1873. Issue: (1) John M.

JOHN M. CAMPBELL, (VIII), Charles Cessna, (VII).

Born November 7, 1874. Occupation, merchant. Address, Salem, Ohio.

RACHEL G. CESSNA, (VI), John (V).

Address, Salem, Ohio. Born, September 21, 1832. Married July 15, 1858, James M. Sears, of Salem, Ohio. Issue: (1) Florence E.

FLORENCE E. SEARS, (VII), Rachel G., (VI).

Address, Salem, Ohio. Born April 16, 1859. Married Emmor Campbell October 19, 1880. Issue: (1) Clara L., (2) James S., (3) Anna F.

CLARA L. CAMPBELL, (VIII), Florence E., (VII).

Born October 21, 1881, died November 3, 1882.

JAMES SEARS CAMPBELL, (VIII), Florence E., (VII).

Born August 10, 1883. Address, Salem, Ohio.

ANNA FRANCIS CAMPBELL (VIII), Florence E. (VII)

Born May 19, 1886.

ALMIRA CESSNA, (VI), John, (V).

Born June 21, 1835, died March 17, 1858.

MARY JANE CESSNA, (VI), John, (V).

Born February 9, 1838, died December 5, 1896. Married John M. Sears, of Salem, Ohio, March 20, 1861. Issue: Rachel Lenora.

122

RACHEL LENORA SEARS, (VII), Mary Jane, (VI).

Born April 6, 1864. Married Charles S. Carr, a merchant of Salem, Ohio, September, 1892. Issue: (1) Florence M., born June 2, 1895. (2) Anna P., born March 24, 1897.

EVALINE CESSNA, (VI), John, (V).

Born September 5, 1840, died July 31, 1898. Married Philo Huxley, of Salem, Ohio, December 17, 1864, a cashier. Issue: (1) Marie Irene, (2) John C., (3) J. Paul.

MARIE IRENE HUXLEY, (VII), Evaline, (VI).

Born January 21, 1867. Married June 1, 1893, Fred H. McClain, of New Castle, Pa., Superintendent Drafting Department, Brown Hoisting Company, Cleveland, Ohio. Issue: (1) John, born August 7, 1896.

JOHN CESSNA HUXLEY, (VII), Evaline, (VI).

Address, Salem, Ohio. Born December 13, 1869. Occupation, Agent for Salem Wire Nail Company. Single.

JARED PAUL HUXLEY, (VII), Evaline, (VI).

Born July 13, 1874. Present Mayor of Salem, Ohio. Married October 29, 1898, Margaret Dow.

MARIA CESSNA, (VI), John, (V).

Born February 18, 1843, died March 17, 1858.

JULIA J. CESSNA, (VI), John, (V)

Born August 1, 1845, died August 23, 1847.

WILLIAM BUTLER CESSNA VI, John v.

Born November 25, 1848. Occupation, farmer. Address, Salem, Ohio. Married (1) Louiza Keeler June 1, 1868. Issue: (1) Belle, (2) John P., (3) Perry Amos. Married (2) Mrs. Elizabeth Masters, August 22, 1878. Issue: (1) Joseph E., (2) Lottie J., (3) James B.

BELLE CESSNA, (VII), William, (VI).

Born April 10, 1869. Address, Salem, Ohio. Married December 31, 1890 William Smith, a farmer. Issue: (1) Harry McConnor, (2) Cessna Amos, (3) Joseph, (4) Edward.

JOHN P. CESSNA, (VII), William, (VI).

Address, Newton Falls, Ohio. Occupation, stock-dealer. Born October 8, 1871. Married Lura Reighard October 15, 1892.

PEERRY AMOS CESSNA, (VII), William, (VI).

Address, Sedalia, Mo. Occupation, Manager McGrew Milling Company. Born December 25, 1873. Married Margaret Lister.

JOSEPH E. CESSNA, (VII), William B., (VI).

Born July 24, 1879. Address, Salem, Ohio.

LOTTIE JANE CESSNA, (VII), William, (VI).

Born December 11, 1883. Address, Salem, Ohio.

JAMES BRYAN CESSNA, (VII), William, (VI).

Born June 26, 1885. Address, Hickory, Ohio.
"John Cessna lived in and around Salem, Ohio, his entire married life. He was a man of good judgment, very

124

successful in accumulating homes for himself and each of his children and economical in all his habits. He was a man of the strictest integrity, full of public spirit, a Jacksonian Democrat, and lived and died respected and honored by all his acquaintances."

SARAH CESSNA V, William iv.

Married William Boor, of Bedford County, Pa. They lived in Sandusky County, Ohio. Samuel Boor, Helena, Ohio, is one of their children. The names of the other children are unknown to the author.

MARGARET CESSNA V, William iv.

Married George Elder. Issue: (1) Joseph, (2) Frank. Address, Buffalo Mills, Pa.

JAMES H. CESSNA V, William iv.

Born about 1815. Married Mary Ann Boor. Issue: (1) John, (2) William, (3) Martin, (4) Joseph, (5) David, (6) Scott, (7) Nancy E., (8) Margaret Ellen, (9) Elizabeth Anna, (10) Collins.

JOHN CESSNA VI, James H.

Address, Rainsburg, Pa. Occupation, retired farmer. Married Miss Bortz. Issue: (1) Carrie, (2) William, (3) John Calvin, (4) Vernon, (5) Wright, drowned at Cumberland, Md.; (6) Daniel.

CARRIE CESSNA, (VII), John, (VI).

Married Mr. Charley Miller, a merchant of Bedford, Pa. She died in 1899.

WILLIAM CESSNA, (VII), John, (VI).

Address, Ellerslie, Md. Married. Age, about 33. Is a railroader.

JOHN CALVIN CESSNA, (VII), John, (VI).

Address, Cumberland, Md. Occupation, salesman. Age, about 30.

VERNON CESSNA, (VII), John, (VI).

Died at the home of his parents in Bedford when about eighteen years of age.

DANIEL CESSNA (VII), John, (VI).

Address, somewhere in Ohio. Was married in 1902.

WILLIAM CESSNA VI, James v.

Address, Grand Island, Neb. Single. Was in the Regular Army for a period of five years. Belonged to the Second U. S. Cavalry.

MARTIN CESSNA VI, Iames v.

Died after returning from prison. Was captured while serving with the Pennsylvania Bucktails in the Civil War.

JOSEPH CESSNA VI, James v.

Born October 10, 1840, died January 25, 1876. Occupation, carpenter. Married Polly Cessna Bruner, who, with her son now lives at Macon, Mo. Issue: (1) Mollie, died young; (2) William.

WILLIAM, (VII), Joseph, (VI).

Address, Macon, Mo. Occupation, harness maker. Born November 27, 1870. Single.

DAVID CESSNA VI, James v.

Occupation, engineer in Michigan.

SCOTT CESSNA, (VI), James, (V).

Occupation, salesman, at Niles, Ohio.

NANCY EVE CESSNA VI, James v.

Married John McCoy, of Cumberland, Md., a boat builder. Issue: (1) Julia, clerk in Philadelphia; (2) Carrie, seamstress.

ELIZABETH CESSNA VI, James v.

Married Daniel Ammon, of Renovo, Pa., an engineer. Issue: (1) Jennie, (2) Daniel.

JONATHAN CESSNA VI, William v.

Born in 1841. Occupation, farmer. Married Elizabeth Karr. Issue: (1) Anna, (2) William K., (3) George E., (4) James, (5) Rachel, (6) John D., (7) Sarah, (8) Joseph P., (9) W. Scott, (10) Jonathan Jackson.

ANN CESSNA VI, Jonathan v.

Born February 2, 1834. Married Levi Luman, of Kansas, Ohio.

W. K. CESSNA VI, Jonathan v.

Address, Gainesville, Florida. Occupation, attorney-at-law. Born December 21, 1835.

GEORGE E. CESSNA, (VI), Jonathan, (V).

Address, Bowling Green, Ohio. Born January 3, 1838.

JAMES H. CESSNA, (VI), Jonathan, (V). (Dead.)

RACHEL CESSNA IV, Jonathan V.

Address, Mindes Mines, Mo. Born March 3, 1843. Married Henry Flock.

JOHN D. CESSNA VI, Jonathan V.

Born October 12. 1844. Residence unknown to author.

JOSEPH P. CESSNA VI, Jonathan V.

Address, Kansas, Ohio. Born April 1, 1847. Married Sarah Snyder. Issue: (1) John, (2) Ralph, (3) Harry. All live at Kansas, Ohio.

SARAH CESSNA VI. Jonathan V.

Address, Kansas, Ohio. Born January 18, 1849. Married George W. Foasel.

JONATHAN JACKSON CESSNA VI, Jonathan V.

Address, Kansas, Ohio. Born February 12, 1852. Married Mary C. Fabing. Issue: (1) Martha E., (2) C. W., (3) Fred. Martha E. Cessna married Birt Michaels.

WINFIELD SCOTT CESSNA VI, Jonathan V.

Born September 7, 1854. (Dead.)

RACHEL CESSNA V, WILLIAM IV.   cR. b 1820
                                           d 1845
Married John D. Cook, of Green County, Ohio.   25 yrs old
bur. Mahoning Co., OH

128

ELIZABETH CESSNA V, WILLIAM IV.

Born 1820. Married Achor Elder, of Cumberland Valley, Pa. Issue: (1) Sarah, (2) Curtis, (3) Emma, (4) William, (5) Jonathan, (6) Horace. She is now living in Bloomdale, Wood County, Ohio.

JOSEPH P. CESSNA V, WILLIAM IV. b. 1904

Born September 29, 1825. Address, Canfield, Ohio. Occupation, physician. Married Lavina Null. Issue: (1) Nancy E., (2) William J., (3) Ledrue R.

Dr. J. P. Cessna was a Surgeon in the army during the Civil War. He has aided much in compiling data for this work.

NANCY E. CESSNA VI, Joseph P. y.

Address, Bellevere, Michigan. Born January 29, 1850. Was an artist. Married D. Albert Adams. Issue: (1) Nellie, born 1875.

WILLIAM J. CESSNA VI, Joseph v.

Address, Battle Creek, Michigan. Born August 3, 1852. Occupation, glazier. Married Irene Faucher. Issue: (1) Otis J., (2) Oliver D.

OTIS J. CESSNA, age 24, a stenographer.

LEDRUE R. CESSNA VI, Joseph v.

Address, Cripple Creek, Colorado. Occupation, salesman. Born May 21, 1857. Married. No issue.

WILLIAM CESSNA V, WILLIAM IV, John iii.

Lived and died in Cumberland Valley, near Centreville, Pa. Was a shoemaker by trade. He lies buried in the old graveyard now owned by Joseph Smith. His grave, and

129

that of his wife, are in the little enclosure near that of Jonathan Cessna's and his two sons, William and Joseph. He married a Miss Snave. Issue: (1) Jacob S., (2) John H., (3) William, (4) George, (5) Amanda, (6) Nancy, (7) Rebecca, (8) Mary, (9) Sarah.

GEORGE CESSNA VI, William V.

Died in 1878. Lived in Tyrone, Pa. Was a policeman. Married (1) Elizabeth Diehl. Issue: (1) John, (2) William.

WILLIAM CESSNA VI, William V.

Lived at Pittsburg, Pa. He has a daughter by the name of Mrs. Mary Strausberry, at Cumberland, Md.

AMANDA CESSNA VI, William V.

Married Nelson Henry, who died at Pittsburg, Pa.

NANCY CESSNA VI, William V,

Married a Mr. Little and lived in Bedford, Pa. Issue: William, Oliver, George, Carrie, Kate.

REBECCA CESSNA VI, William V.

Married a Mr. Ray, who died at Hyndman, Pa.

MARY CESSNA VI, William V.

Married a Mr. Rickle, of Altoona, Pa. Issue: Margaret, Naomi.

SARAH CESSNA VI, William V

Married a Mr. Ruddleson, a wheelwright of Iowa.

JOHN H. CESSNA VI, William v.

Married Mary Diehl. Issue: (1) Ella, (2) A. J. Burton, (3) Franklin Kremer. Address, Altoona, Pa.

Prof. John H. Cessna was County Superintendent of Bedford County schools. Franklin, the youngest son died from the effects of an injury received in a foot-ball game at Lancaster where he was attending Franklin and Marshall College with the ministry in view.

JACOB S. CESSNA VI, William V, William IV, John iii.

Address, Centreville, Pa. Farmer, born about 1834. Married Mary E. Krickvaum. Issue: (1) Alice E., (2) Tom H. Benton, (3) Mary E., (4) John K., (5) Henry A., (6) Charles Alvin, (7) Clara V., (8) Edgar G., (9) Herbert Leslie.

ALICE E. CESSNA, (VIII), Jacob S., (VI).

Address, Cumberland, Md. Born about 1858. Married William Gilliam. Issue: Harry B.

TOM H. BENTON CESSNA, (VII), Jacob, (VI).

Address, Ellerslie, Md. Born about 1861. Married Emma Hite. Issue: (1) Wayne, age 11; (2) Carl, age 6.

MARY E. CESSNA, (VII), Jacob S., (VI).

Address, Centreville, Pa. Born about 1864. Married John Warmuth. Issue: (1) William S., age 17; (2) Earl, age 14; (3) Eliza, (4) Clyde.

JOHN K. CESSNA, (VII), Jacob S., (VI).

Address, Mt. Savage, Md. Born 1866. Married Cora V. Hendrickson. Issue: (1) Ralph, age 12; (2) John, (3) Raymond.

HENRY A. CESSNA, (VII), Jacob S., (VI).

Address, Johnstown, Pa. Teacher. Born 1871. Single.

CLARA V. CESSNA, (VII), Jacob S., (VI).

Address, Six Mile Run, Pa. Born 1875. Married Prof. James G. Jamison.

EDWARD G. CESSNA, (VII), Jacob S., (VI).

Address, Mt. Savage, Md. Born 1877. Single.

HERBERT CESSNA, (VII), Jacob S., (VI).

Address Mt. Savage, Md. Born 1880. Single.

BIOGRAPHY OF SUPT. JOHN H. CESSNA

John H. Cessna, the subject of this biographical sketch, was born in Cumberland Valley township, Bedford County, Pa., near the village of Centerville, on June 15, 1839. His father was William Cessna. His mother died when he was about two years old. A few years later his father undertook to move west in a wagon, but got no farther than Westmoreland County, Pa., where he lived a couple of years and then returned to Bedford, Pa. The boy was put among relatives in Juniata township, Bedford County, and later among relatives in Somerset County to "paddle his own canoe." His first day at school was in the log school house near Burns Mills, now Fyan's Mills, Juniata township, Bedford County. He lived in Somerset County two or three years when his father brought him back to Bedford, and put him to live with Mr. Matthew Pearson's family, near the town of Wolfsburg, Bedford township. He lived at Pearson's about two years and then went to Friend's Cove, and worked among the farmers, receiving seven or eight dollars per month for his labor.

PROF. JOHN H. CESSNA.
Page 92.

134

When he was about sixteen years of age he went to learn
the carpenter trade with Mr. Conrad Feaster, of Schellsburg, Pa. He served an apprenticeship of three years with
Mr. Feaster. Up to this time he had gone to school but a
very few months and could barely read and write. He
found he could not make the calculations necessary to carry
on his trade. So he went to a public school in the "Dutch
Corner," making his home with Mr. Thomas Imler, for
whom he had helped to build a large barn the previous
summer, working mornings and evenings and on Saturdays
to pay for his boarding. In the Spring of 1860 he attended
the Allegheny Male and Female Seminary at Rainsburg,
Pa., which at that time was the best and most flourishing
school in the county. He got along so well and learned so
rapidly that his friends advised him to apply for a school
as teacher. This he did and commenced teaching in the
Charlesville school, Colerain township, in the Fall of 1860.
He continued to teach the same school during four months
in the Winter, his wages being twenty dollars per month,
and went to school during the summer until the war broke
the school up in 1863. In 1862 he offered to go to the army
but was rejected at Harrisburg, on account of physical disability. He was afterward drafted three times, but never
got into the army. For several years he taught school
during the Winter and worked at the Carpenter trade during the Summer, until he became physically unable to work
at his trade. He then sought better positions in teaching.
He taught as principal of the Schellsburg, Saxton and
Everett schools, and during the vacations taught classes of
teachers in different parts of the county—studying all the
time—until 1881, when he was elected County Superintendent. This office he filled with credit to himself and much
profit to the schools of the county, for nine years. By his
untiring energy and indefatagable labor, he infused a life
and enthusiasm into the school work of the county, which
gave it an impetus, heretofore not experienced. In 1892
he was elected to supervise—with close supervision—the
schools of Logan township, Blair County, Pa., with his

office in Altoona city. He had charge of those schools during the school term, and represented the American Book Company, of New York, during his vacations, in the counties of Huntingdon, Bedford, Fulton, Juniata, Lebanon, and sometimes going into Chester, Berks and Bucks, until 1898, when he quit the school work entirely, and engaged with the Christopher Sower Publishing Company, of Philadelphia, to represent the interests of the company in all the northwestern part of Pennsylvania and parts of Maryland and West Virginia, which position he still holds. He is widely known among educators, school people and book men all over the State, and is regarded as a strong book man.

SQUIRE JAMES CESSNA iv, JOHN iii

Married (1) Miss Lysinger. Issue: (1) John J., (2) Charles, (3) Alexander, (4) William, (5) Polly, (6) Susan, (7) Margaret. Married (2) Miss Miller. Issue: (1) James Buchanan, (2) Jonathan, (3) Wilson, (4) Samuel, (5) Henry, (6) Alsinda.

SHERIFF JOHN J. CESSNA V, James IV.

Married Nancy Powell. Died December, 1891, age 73. Occupation, tailor, constable, liveryman, Sheriff. Issue: (1) John A., (2) William S., (3) James P., (4) Mary E., (5) Frank P.

JOHN A. CESSNA iv, John J. v.

Born May 17, 1842. Occupation, liveryman. Was Coroner, Deputy Sheriff under Henderson, Keyser and Eicholtz. Assessor in Bedford for the past ten years. Married Minna Keyser. Issue: (1) Charles W., (2) Maggie K., (3) Ada M., (4) J. Roy, (5) Marcy F.

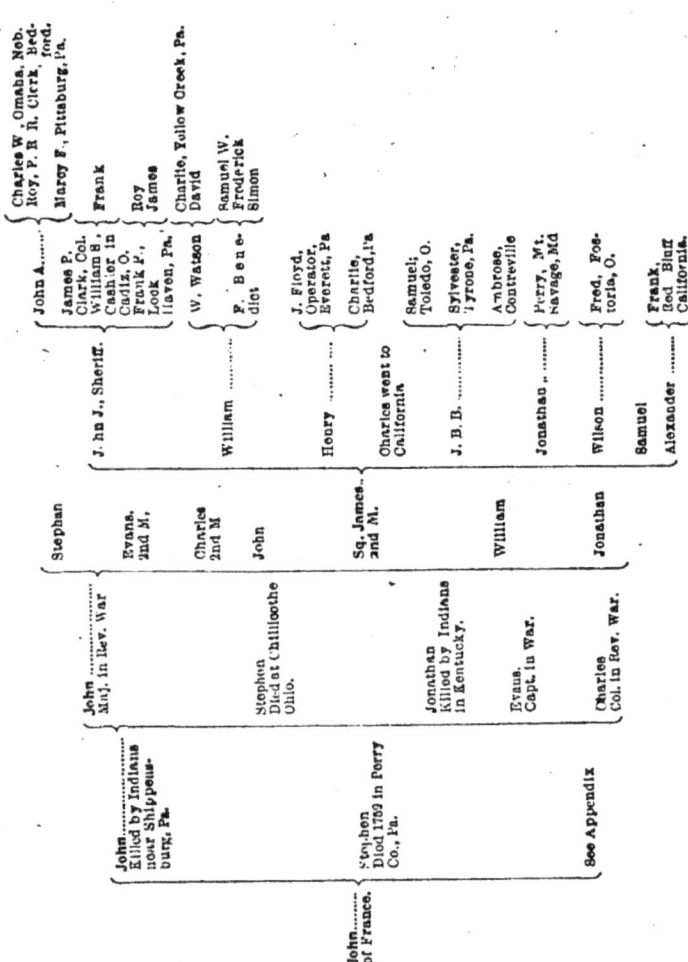

CHARLES W. CESSNA, (VII), John A., (VI).

Born February 22, 1866. Occupation, manager of theatre at Omaha, Neb., is an operator. Married a lady from Omaha, Neb.

MAGGIE K. CESSNA, (VII), John A., (VI).

Address, Bedford, Pa. Married A. J. Allen, a chair manufacturer and grocer. Issue: (1) Ruth, (2) Charles, (3) Nancy, (4) Roy.

ADA M. CESSNA, (VII), John A., (VI).

Address, Hyndman, Pa. Married Charles R. Rhodes, a druggist. Issue: Ethel.

J. ROY CESSNA, (VII), John A., (VI).

Address, Bedford, Pa. Born 1872. Single. Occupation, Clerk for Superintendent of Bedford Division P. R. R. Co.

MARCY F. CESSNA, (VII), John A., (VI).

Address, Pittsburg, Pa. Born 1874. Single. Occupation, clerk.

WILLIAM S. CESSNA VI, John J. v.

Address, Cadiz, Ohio. Born about 1844. Occupation, cashier of First National Bank. Has been cashier for sixteen years. Married, Laura McBane, daughter of Dr. McBane, of Cadiz, Ohio. Issue: Frank, age 19.

JAMES P. CESSNA VI, John J. v.

Address, Clark, Colorado. Occupation, stockman. Was Justice of the Peace and postmaster in Clark. Single.

138

MARY E. CESSNA VI, John J.v.

Address, Sioux City, Iowa. Married William Dorsey, a merchant. Issue: (1) May, (2) Helen, (3) Minna.

FRANK P. CESSNA VI, John J. v.

Address, Lock Haven, Pa. Born about 1850. Occupation, cigar manufacturer. Married Mary Ray. Issue: (1) Ray, (2) James, (3) Carrie, (4) Ethel.

J. B. B. CESSNA V, SQUIRE JAMES IV, John iii.

Born September 28, 1838. Address, Cumberland Valley, Pa. Married Margaret Elliott. Issue: (1) Sylvester, (2) Samuel B., (3) Blanche, (4) Ambrose.

SAMUEL CESSNA VI, J. B. B. v.

Address, Toledo, Ohio. Married Emma Wertz. Occupation, oil dealer.

AMBROSE CESSNA VI, J. B. B.v.

Address, Centreville, Pa. Married. Issue. (1) Sardus Alton, (2) Susan Pearl.

SYLVESTER CESSNA VI, J. B. B. v.

Address, Tyrone, Pa. Railroader.

HENRY CESSNA V, JAMES IV.

Married Jennie Reichard. Died a few years ago at about fifty years of age. Was a stone cutter by occupation. Issue: John Floyd, (2) Elizabeth Bessie, (3) Charlie, (4) May Lulu.

139

J. FLOYD CESSNA VI, HENRY V.

Address, Everett, Pa. Occupation, operator. Married Minnie Bulger. Issue: (1) Mildren E.

BESSIE CESSNA VI, Henry v.

Address, Pittsburg, Pa. Married John Prosser, a clerk.

CHARLIE CESSNA VI, Henry v.

Address, Bedford, Pa. Single.

MAY LULU CESSNA VI, Henry v.

Address, Bedford, Pa. Single.

JONATHAN CESSNA V, SQUIRE JAMES IV, John III.

Married Fannie Wood. Issue: (1) Perry, (2) Ocra. Address, Mt. Savage, Md. Has in his possession a hickory cane presented to Jonathan (IV) by President Jackson.

SAMUEL CESSNA V, SQUIRE JAMES IV.

Married Annie Miller. Address, Centreville, Pa. Has a part of Major John Cessna's uniform in his possession.

WILSON CESSNA V, SQUIRE JAMES IV.

Address, Fostoria, Ohio. Married. Issue. Fred. Occupation, oil dealer.

WILLIAM CESSNA V, JAMES IV

Married Margaret Shearer. Issue: (1) F. Benedick, (2) W. Watson, (3) Mary. Died about 1895 aged 67. Was in the Civil War. Returned from the war one day after his wife's death. Was a strong man until he fell on a load of ice. Was an invalid from that time until his death some years later.

F. BENEDICK CESSNA VI, William v.

Born February 29, 1856. Married Annie Steele. Issue: (1) Samuel W., (2) Della, (3) Frederick, (4) Lena, (5) Simon. Address, Yellow Creek, Pa. Occupation, merchant.

W. WATSON CESSNA VI, William v, Squire James iv.

Address, Yellow Creek, Pa. Born April 16, 1854. Married (1) Mary Burket. Issue: (1) Elizabeth, (2) Charles, (3) Annie, (4) David, born 1885.

MARY CESSNA VI, William v.

Address, Reading, Pa. Born 1858. Married Tony Crouse.

EVAN CESSNA IV. JOHN III, JOHN II, John I.

Born October 2, 1791. Married a Miss Helsel, of Dutch Corner, Bedford County, Pa. Issue: (1) Samuel, (2) Elizabeth, (3) William, (4) Matilda, (5) Sarah, (6) James, (7) John, (8) Mary.

Evan Cessna at one time lived in Everett, Pa. He was rather a large man. He had a shop near where Mr. Messersmith now has one. He was a good shot with a rifle. He went blind and moved to Ohio about 1840. His brother, Charles Cessna, was a very strong man.

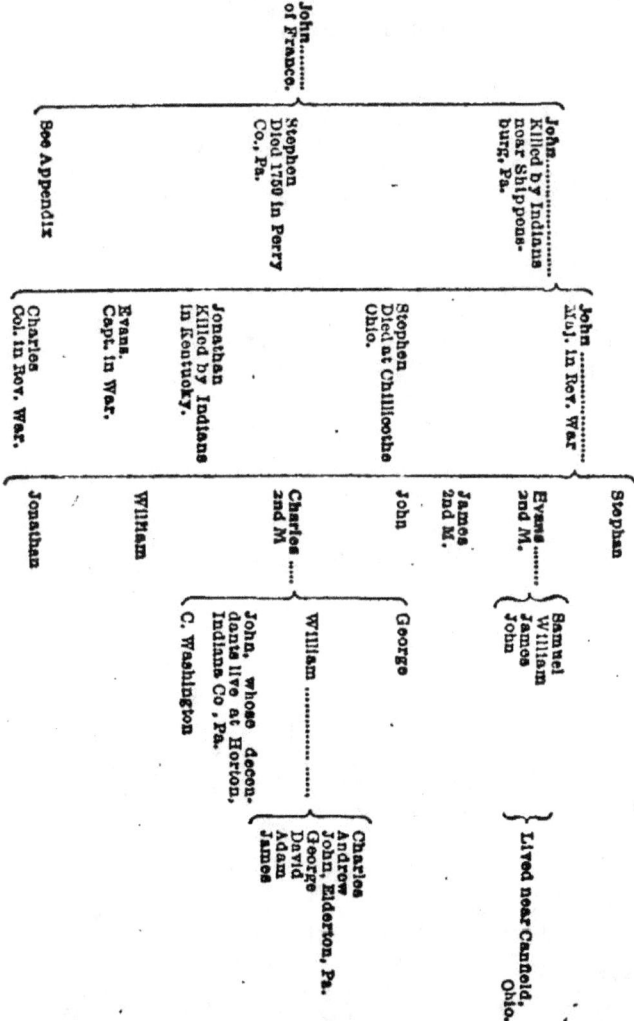

John...... of France.

See Appendix

John...... Killed by Indians near Shippens- burg, Pa.

Stephen Died 1759 in Perry Co., Pa.

John ...... Maj. in Rev. War

Charles Col. in Rev. War.

Evan, Capt. in War.

Jonathan Killed by Indians in Kentucky.

Stephen Died at Chillicothe Ohio.

James 2nd M.

Evans .... { William James John

Stephan

Jonathan

William

Charles .....

John

Samuel William James John

George

C. Washington

William ....

John, whose descen- dants live at Horton, Indiana Co., Pa.

Lived near Canfield, Ohio.

Charles Andrew John, Elderton, Pa. George David Adam James

142

SARAH CESSNA V, EVAN IV.

Married Jacob Dustman. Issue: (1) William, of Cleveland, Ohio; (2) Frank, of Limaville, Ohio; (3) Rosa Hahn, of Limaville, Ohio; (4) John, of Limaville, Ohio; (5) James, of Berlin, Ohio; (6) Mary Dustman, of Berlin, Ohio.

MATILDA CESSNA V, EVAN IV.

Married William Crouk, of Canfield, Ohio. Issue: (1) Jefferson, of Lordstown, Ohio; (2) William A., of Canfield, Ohio; (3) Elizabeth, of Berlin, Ohio.

MARY CESSNA V EVAN IV.

Married John Swartz, of Alliance, Ohio.

WILLIAM CESSNA V, EVAN IV.

Address is thought to be Champion County, Illinois.

CHARLES CESSNA IV, JOHN III, JOHN II, John I.

Born March 10, 1789. Married Katie Smouse. Died at Blairsville, Indiana County, Pa., about 1829. Issue: (1) George, (2) William, (3) Elizabeth, (4) John, (5) Annie, (6) Peggie, (7) Polly, (8) C. Washington.

WILLIAM CESSNA V, CHARLES IV

Married Elizabeth Bowers. Issue: (1) Charles, (2) Andrew, (3) Barbara, (4) John, (5) George, (6) David, (7) Nancy, (8) Adam, (9) James, (10) Mary, (11) Rachel.

John (VI) lives in Elderton, Pa. Andrew (VI) lives in Adams County, Ohio. Rachel (VI) lives in Johnstown, Pa.

Nephews of William (V) by the names of G. W. Cessna

and Milton E. Cessna live at Horton, Indiana County, Pa. John Cessna (VI), of Elderton, Pa., gave me the above information, and owing to his cousins not answering letters was unable to give particulars of uncles families.

Stephen Cissna III, John II.

Came from Pennsylvania. Was married to Elizabeth Barnhill, who was also from Pennsylvania. He served in the Revolutionary War. Lived at Chillocothe, Ohio, died and was buried there with honors of war.

MILITARY RECORD OF STEPHEN CESSNA III.

In June and July, 1775, nine companies of expert riflemen were raised in Pennsylvania known, first, as the Battalion of Riflemen; second, First Pennsylvania Regiment. The battalion was ordered to march to Boston and there join the American army. The pay of the privates was six and two-third dollars, to find their own arms and clothes. Every regiment had a standard and colors. The standard of the Battalion of Riflemen or First Regiment is now in the possession of the State of Pennsylvania, having been purchased by Hon. M. S. Quay from Thomas Robinson, Esq., grandson of Lieutenant Colonel Thomas Robinson of the First Pennsylvania. It is a deep green ground, the device, a tiger partly enclosed by toils, attempting the pass, defended by a hunter armed with a spear (in white) on crimson field, the motto "Domari nolo." This regiment of riflemen, it appears from information contained in Vol. 10, Pa. Archives, second series, was used as sharp shooters.

Stephen Cessna enlisted in this regiment in Capt. Robert Cluggage's company. See Vol 10, Pa. Archives, p. 18, second series.

After the war ended Capt. Cluggage lived in Hunting-

Georgia King,
Kansas City, Mo.

George King ....
Charles Miller

Stephen ....
Williamsport Ind.
William
Clissa Park, Ind.

Stephen ....
War of 1812

Charles
Portsmouth, Ohio.

Joseph
St. Louis, Mo.

Baldwin
Chillicothe, Ohio.

George
Chillicothe, Ohio.

John
Maj. in Rev. War

Stephen ....
Died at Chillicothe
Ohio.

Jonathan
Killed by Indians
in Kentucky.

Evans
Capt. in War.

Charles
Col. in Rev. War.

John ....
Killed by Indians
near Shippens-
burg, Pa.

Stephen
Died 1769 in Perry
Co., Pa.

See Appendix

John ....
of France.

COMMENTARY: Stephen Cissna of Chillicothe, OH

In his first House of Cessna book, Howard reports that Stephen Cissna who fought with Washington as a Rifleman, and died in Chillicothe, OH was a son of John II. (Roman numerals after the name were used by Howard to indicate generation.) However, in his will John II does not mention Stephen among his children. Closer inspection of the family tree indicates that John's son Evan was born in the same year as the Stephen being referred to.

Stephen Cissna of Chillicothe records his date of birth as July 1755. This matches the Stephen who is born to Thomas and Margaret Cesna in Carlisle, PA and christened in September of that year. Patience Cisney records that he is the grandson of her and Stephen.

Please see note these references:

Baptism note of pastor of St. James Church in Lancaster: baptism which took place in Carlisle, Sept 15, 1755, Stephen Sisney, s/o Thomas and Margaret Sisney.

Cumberland County Orphan's Court: August 1763, Patience Sisney comes asking for guardianship of the inheritance (from her husband Stephen) due her grandchildren: Stephen and John Sisney s/o her son John; and Stephen Sisney s/o her son Thomas; during their minority. William Smith is appointed guardian.

Family records indicate that the Stephen we are discussing was raised in the household of John II, but the will does not list him as a son. It is not hard to imagine that the orphaned boy was adopted by his great uncle after both parents died. His mother Margaret Gallacher-Cisney married James Hamilton on 30 November 1763 and died within a year of that marriage. Stephen was orphaned at 8 years of age.

146

don County, Pa., was Justice of the Peace. (I infer that this Stephen Cessna was a brother of Maj. John Cessna.)

In the same volume above referred to, page 345, the name Stephen Cisne again appears as serving in Maj. James Moore's company—seven months' men belonging to the First Pennsylvania regiment. Without a doubt this Stephen Cisne is the same person who enlisted in Capt. Cluggage's company five years previous.

Thacher in his "Military Journal of the Revolution," under date of August, 1775, describes the Battalion of Riflemen: "They are remarkably stout and hardy men; many of them exceeding six feet in height. They are dressed in white frocks, or rifle shirts, and round hats. These men are remarkable for the accuracy of their aim; striking a mark with great certainty at two hundred yards distance. At a review, a company of them, while on a quick advance fired their balls into objects of seven inches diameter, at the distance of two hundred and fifty yards. They are now stationed in our lines, and their shot have frequently proved fatal to British officers and soldiers who expose themselves to view, even at more than double the distance of common musket shot."

This regiment did service in the engagements around Boston, took part in the Battle of Long Island, Brandywine, et al.

The letters written by the officers and printed in Vol. 10, Pa. Archives, will give the doings of this regiment from the beginning of the war until the ending.

In Bedford County History p. 83, gives doing in full of the regiment to which Stephen Cessna belonged.

Stephen Cissna IV, Stephen III.

Lived in Chillocothe, Ohio. Was married to Sarah King. Two sons were born to them, Stephen and William. He was in the war of 1812. Was wounded in the arm. Same bullet struck a man named English in the breast, also

147

a Frenchman, name unknown to the writer, had a lock of his whiskers shot away by same bullet. None were killed and none seriously wounded. (Do not know what battle this happened in.) Stephen died and was buried at Clarksburg, Ohio.

WILLIAM CESSNA IV, STEPHEN III.

Lived at Chillocothe, Ohio. Went to Natches, Tenn., and it is supposed died there.

Charles ~~MARY~~ CESSNA IV STEPHEN III.

Lived at Chillocothe, Ohio, and is supposed to have lived afterward at or near Portsmouth, Ohio., and at one time owned a large farm near Piketon, Ohio. (Nothing further known.)

JOSEPH CESSNA IV, STEPHEN III.

Lived at Chillocothe, Ohio. Married and went to St. Louis, Mo. (Nothing further known.)

Boaldin BALDWIN CESSNA IV, STEPHEN III.

Lived, died and was buried at Chillocothe, Ohio. Was not married.

GEORGE CESSNA IV STEPHEN III.

Lived at Chillocothe, Ohio. (Nothing more known.)

ELIZABETH CESSNA IV, STEPHEN III.

Lived at Chillocothe, Ohio. Married John Fenimore.

MARY CESSNA IV STEPHEN III.

Lived at Chillocothe, Ohio. Married Thomas Jones and went to St. Louis, Mo.

148

MELINDA CISSNA IV, STEPHEN III.

Lived at Chillocothe, Ohio. Married John Renshaw and went to Bellville, Ill., east of St. Louis, Mo.

ELEANOR CISSNA IV, STEPHEN III.

Lived at Chillocothe, Ohio. Married Samuel Porter and went to St. Louis, Mo., to live.

STEPHEN CISSNA V STEPHEN IV.

Was born at Chillocothe, Ohio, February 9, 1815. Went to Clarksburg, Ohio, thence to Columbus, Ohio, thence to Lafayette, Ind., thence to Williamsport, Ind., where he was married on the 13th of April, 1848, to Elizabeth A. Miller, daughter of Frances Coggswell Buell Miller and Lazarus Miller, and went to live on a farm near Williamsport. Three children were born to them, Sarah Frances, George King, Charles Miller. The first named is the only one now living. He moved to a farm near Ash Grove, Ill., called "Pigeon Grove Farm," thence to a farm near Watseka, Ill., thence to Watseka, where he now resides.

WILLIAM CISSNA V, STEPHEN IV.

Was born at Chillocothe, Ohio, June 17, 1816. Lived at Clarksburg, Ohio, Columbus, Ohio, Lafayette, Ind., Williamsport, Ind., on a farm near "Crows Grove." Went on a farm near Watseka, thence to "Pigeon Grove Farm." Here he founded the town of "Cissna Park," and lived in the town until his death, on February 25, 1895. Was never married.

SARAH FRANCES CISSNA VI, Stephen v.

Was born at Williamsport, Ind., January 28, 1849. Always lived with her father and is now living at Watseka, Ill.

GEORGE KING CISSNA VI, Stephen v.

Was born at Williamsport, Ind., June 17, 1851. Was married in Denver, Colo., to Eva Wright October 7th, died of heart disease on the 9th and was buried at his home in Watseka, Ill., on October 14, 1879.

CHARLES MILLER CISSNA VI, Stephen v.

Was born at Williamsport, Ind., April 3, 1854, died at 22 months of age, and was buried at Williamsport, Ind.

GEORGIA KING CISSNA, (VII), George K, (VI).

Was born at Watseka July 9, 1881. Is now living with her mother, Eva Webster, at Kansas City, Mo.

John A. Cissna, of Lawrenceville, Ill, is a descendant of Stephen IV.

BIOGRAPHY OF STEPHEN CESSNA V

From the Watseka (Ill.) Republican.

Mr. Stephen Cissna died at his home in Watseka, Ill., Wednesday evening at 5.30 o'clock, April 25, 1900, at the age of 85 years, 2 months and 16 days, as the result from a fall sustained a few months ago. Stephen Cissna was born at Chillocothe, Ross County, Ohio, February 9, 1815, and was the son of Stephen Cissna, who was a soldier under Hull in the war of 1812. Mr. Cissna's grandfather, Stephen Cissna, and four sons were soldiers in the Revolutionary War. At 16 years of age Mr. Cissna commenced to learn the trade of tanner in Chillocothe. From there he went to Clarksburg and Columbus, Ohio, where he was engaged in working at his trade. In 1836 he went to Lafayette, Ind., and worked at his trade a short time. In 1837 he commenced farming in Warren County, near Williamsport, Ind., and from that he embarked in the mercantile business in Williamsport, Ind., where he remained for some five years. In 1856 Mr. Cissna came to Iroquois, Ill., and located in Pigeon Grove township on a farm of 680 acres. In 1867 he moved onto a farm three and one-half miles northeast of Watseka, which he had purchased from his brother, William Cissna, where he lived until about sixteen years ago when he moved to Watseka where he resided until his death. Stephen Cissna was married April 13, 1848, to Miss Elizabeth A. Miller, at Williamsport, Ind. She died August 2, 1858. Mr. Cissna was married again November 6, 1864, to Miss Clara Hawk, of Erie, Pa., who survives him. He had three children by his first wife, Sarah Frances, George King, Charles Miller, Sarah Frances alone survives.

"Uncle Cissna," as he was familiarly known, had many friends, in

STEPHEN CISSNA.
Page 104.

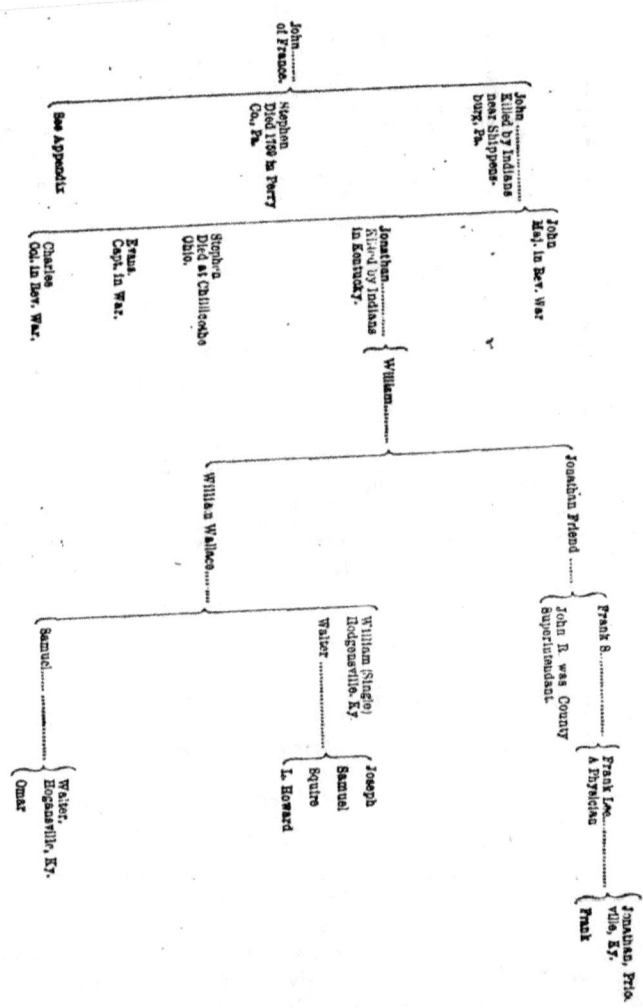

fact every one who knew him was his friend. Kind hearted, generous almost to a fault, he was loved by young and old alike. When he fell and injured himself a few months ago, many were the expressions of sorrow heard from all parts of the town. When it became known that he would probably not recover, it was hoped that his sufferings would be less intense and that his final ending would be peaceful. Mr. Cissna's life is a record of the privations and hardships of pioneer life. He has fought a good fight, he has finished his course, peace be to his ashes. Funeral services will be held at the residence at 2 o'clock p. m. to-day (Friday) conducted by Rev. Stocking assisted by Rev. B. S. Fenall, followed by interment at Oak Hill cemetery.

BIOGRAPHY OF WILLIAM CESSNA V

From the Watseka (Ill.) Republican.

William Cissna, founder of the town of "Cissna Park," Iroquois County, Ill., and well known throughout this section of the country, departed this life Monday, February 25, 1895, of heart failure, aged 79 years. Services were held at Cissna Park, where he resided at the time of his death and the remains wer brought to Watseka, Ill., arriving at 3 o'clock p. m., interment taking place at Oak Hill cemetery, Rev. R. B. Williams conducted the burial services.

Mr. Cissna was born at Chillocotne, Ohio, June 17, 1816. After he was grown he removed to Lafayette, Ind., from there went to Williamsport, Ind., from there to Watseka, Ill., in 1864 where he purchased land northeast of town, now known as the Cissna farm. Two years after he removed to Pigeon Grove, where he founded Cissna Park, where he resided until the time of his death. He was a man generally respected and looked up to as a leader in the community. He had large real estate interests in and about Cissna Park, and elsewhere, and was reputed to be worth considerable over $100,000. He leaves a brother, Stephen Cissna, of this city, and a half sister, Mrs. Rose, of Cissna Park, and two half brothers, George and Noah, Justice of Lafayette, Ind.

Jonathan Cessna iii, John ii.
John i.

Married Mary Friend, of Friend's Cove, Bedford County, Pa. Issue: William.

In Pennsylvania Archives Vol. 14, second series, Jonathan Cessna (III) appears as having served in the Undesignated Militia on duty in 1782. For a while his brother, Evan Cessna, was captain of this company.

The following letter received from one of the descendants of Jonathan Cessna (III) gives in detail the early history of the Cessnas in Kentucky:

153

HODGENSVILLE, Ky., May 18, 1899.

Mr. Howard Cessna,
      Bedford, Pa.

    Dear Sir:—After a delay which could not possibly have been averted, I avail myself of the first opportunity in the pleasure of replying to your esteemed letter of former date relating to the history of the Cessna family. As I believe I have prior to this time given you some statistics regarding the family in Kentucky, I will on this occasion give you the facts as briefly as possible to be correct. While history loves to linger on the many noble deeds of bravery and romance that stand prominently in the early settlement of our Old Kentucky Home, there is no name more honorably interwoven in her settlement and history of a sister State than the name Cessna. In falling the timbers of the forest and causing the roses to bloom in their stead, in driving back the savage Indians and in planting the school house and church where riot and bloodshed ruled supreme, in substituting civilization for heathenism no name is more prominently associated than the name Cessna. In the lawmaking, judiciary and executive functions of Kentucky none have contributed more honorably. Somewhere about 1775 Jonathan Cessna, who was formerly married to Mary Friend, of Friend's Cove, Pa., emigrated from there to Kentucky, where Louisville now stands on the banks of the Ohio River, cleared two acres of land, the first land cleared within the limits of the metropolis. Soon after he was killed by the Indians leaving one son, William, aged three years, who remembered the last time he saw his father by the following incident: The whites having made preparations to go out on an Indian raid, had collected on the banks of the Ohio River, at what is now Louisville, to execute their intention. Jonathan took his son, William, in his arms, kissed him good-bye and told him to be a good boy and obey his mother. He never returned

154

to his pleasant cabin home or his beloved family, but was numbered with the slain after the bloody war was over.

During William's boyhood, he and his mother emigrated south about 65 miles, near the present town of Hodgensville, the county seat of LaRue County, (terminus of the Illinois Central Railroad) and took up a large tract of land, some of which is still in the possession of the Cessna family. William was successful in his day as a farmer and financier, having amassed a considerable fortune. He was married to Sally Wallace, who was born in Edinburg, Scotland, and came to this country and to Kentucky when twelve years old with her parents. Her father by birth was a descendant of the distinguished Knight of Scotland, Sir William Wallace. William was elected by the Democratic party in the year —— being the first representative LaRue County had in the General Assembly of Kentucky. He was re-elected and served the second term.

WILLIAM CESSNA IV, JONATHAN III.

He was born in 1776 and died in 1866. His wife preceded him thirty years. Their union was blessed with nine children, to wit: (1) Margaret, died in infancy; (2) Jonathan Friend, (3) Betsy, (4) Mary, (5) Nancy, (6) Matilda, (7) Susan, (8) Margaret, (9) William Wallace.

JONATHAN FRIEND CESSNA V, WILLIAM IV, Jonathan III.

Was born November 16, 1804. Was married to Nancy Miller, of Hodgensville, Ky., February 14, 1832, died May 19, 1885. His wife preceded him thirty-five years. She died October 15, 1850. He began life as a farmer but his strong native intelligence and honorable aspirations brought him before the public. The first position of trust to which he was called was that of Sheriff of LaRue County in 1843. Early in life he began the study of law, was admitted to the bar and won an enviable reputation as an attorney. In 1854 he was elected to the office of county Judge, the duties of which he discharged with integrity and ability. He was re-elected and in all served twelve years. In 1872 he was nominated by the Democracy of this district for State Senator, but owing to dissatisfaction in the party was defeated by a small majority. He was always a Democrat and his political affiliations were never known to waver. He was a consistent member of the Baptist Church and also prominent in Masonry. Issue: Five sons and three daughters. Three sons died in infancy. The names of those who lived to be grown are Mary Elizabeth, Francis Stuart, Sarah, Nanie, John Rowan.

BETSY CESSNA V, William IV, Jonathan III.

Married John C. Williams, a farmer of Hodgensville, Kentucky.

MARY CESSNA V, William IV, Jonathan iii.

Married John T. Hodges, a farmer of Bloomfield, Ky.

NANCY CESSNA V, William IV, Jonathan iii.

Married I. M. Wooten, a farmer of Bloomfield, Ky.

MATILDA CESSNA V, William IV, Jonathan iii.

Married James Rust, a sadler of Hodgensville, Ky.

MARGARET CESSNA V, William IV, Jonathan iii.

Married Harry Fisher, a farmer of Hodgensville, Ky.

SUSAN CESSNA, (V), William, (IV), Jonathan, (III).

Married Joseph Walters, a farmer of Hodgensville, Ky.

WILLIAM WALLACE CESSNA V, William IV, Jonathan iii.

Married the Widow Quinn, formerly Marion Wallace Coombs. Farmer William died June, 1855.

MARY E. VI, Jonathan v, William iv.

Married John Durham, a farmer of Hodgensville, Ky. Issue: William Cessna, Nannie Shreve.

FRANK S. CESSNA VI. Jonathan v, William iv.

Was born May 12, 1835, died October 12, 1886. Was married to Sarah E. Hays May 25, 1858. He joined the Baptist Church in 1855, was ordained to preach June 27, 1861. His time was not always exclusively devoted to preaching, a matter he often regretted. At intervals a part of his time was devoted to teaching. At different times he was Common School Commissioner of LaRue County, which office he held at the time of his death. He was exceedingly modest and retiring, yet his purity of character and his gentle and amiable disposition always rendered him respected and popular. It was said by many who knew him when he died that a good man had entered upon a peaceful and happy reward, and is missed in his family, in his church, in his community, in his county and in the Association. Issue: Nannie Truman, Frank Lee, Margaret Alice.

SARAH CESSNA VI, Jonathan v, William iv.

Not married.

NANNIE CESSNA VI, Jonathan v, William iv.

Married S. G. Elliott, a blacksmith of Hodgensville, Ky. Issue: William Eldred, Hallie Cessna, Maud Hubbard, Eula Lee.

JOHN R. CESSNA VI, Jonathan v. William iv.

Married Maggie V. Marshall April 20, 1886. He was born March 9, 1848, died May 7, 1894. J. R. Cessna was one of the most popular and highly respected citizens of Hodgensville. He at all times took a warm interest in all mat-

157

ters connected with church and education. He was a school teacher for several years and afterward became Superintendent of the County Schools, which office he held at his death. He had served two terms giving general satisfaction in the conduct of his office. He was a member of the Baptist Church and for years served as Church Clerk; also Superintendent of Sunday School. He was sadly missed by the members of his congregation and by the te hers of the county. Issue: Florence Edmonia, Mary Margaret.

NANNIE TRUMAN CESSNA, (VII), Frank S., (VI), Jonathan, (V).

Married Ernest Miller, of Louisville, Ky. Issue: Frankie, Bettie Hite.

DR. FRANK LEE CESSNA, (VII), Frank S., (VI), Jonathan, (V).

Married Mary Rowe, of Priceville, Ky. He is a member of the Baptist Church and by his many virtues and good qualifications has won for himself a great reputation and a large practice. Issue: Jonathan Rowe, Frank.

ALLIE CESSNA, (VII), Frank S., (VI), Jonathan, (V).

Married George Kirkpatrick June 9, 1886, died July 24, 1888, Hodgensville. No children.

FLORENCE EDMONIA CESSNA, (VII), John B., (VI), Jonathan, (V).

Married Joseph Howard, a farmer. Issue: John Cessna, Vernon.

WILLIAM CESSNA VI, William V, William iv, Jonathan iii.

Born 1854. Address, Hodgensville, Ky. Single.

JUDGE JONATHAN CESSNA.
Pages 111 to 113.

159

WALTER CESSNA VI, William V, William iv.

Born 1856. Address, Hodgensville, Ky. Occupation, stockman and county clerk. Married Sudie Walters. Issue: (1) Joseph, (2) Mary, (3) Samuel, (4) Squire, (6) Leslie Howard.

SAMUEL CESSNA VI, William V, William iv.

Born 1859. Address, Hodgensville, Ky. Married Emma Weissinger. Issue: (1) Walter, (2) Eva, (3) Irene, (4) Omar.

The following is a history of the life of Judge Jonathan Cessna, of Kentucky:

A meeting of the Hodgenville Bar and officers of LaRue County was called at Hodgenville, on the 22d day of May, 1885, to pass resolutions upon the death of Judge J. F. Cessna. Dr. W. H Hamilton was elected Chairman and G. W. Thursman Secretary. I. W. Twyman, G. W. Thurman, H. S. Johnson, J. W. Gore and J. E. Wight were appointed a committee on resolutions and they submitted the following, which were adopted, to wit:

WHEREAS, By the decree of Divine Providence Judge J. F. Cessna has been called from our midst to a blissful home beyound the grave. Therefore, be it

RESOLVED, First, That whilst we fully recognize and highly appreciate his kindly association, his eminent attainments and his honorable and just administration as a jurist, his well kown integrity as a lawyer, his just and upright conduct as a public officer, his honesty, uprightness and purity of life as a private citizen, we bow with humility to the decree of the Supreme Ruler of the Universe in taking from us a beloved friend, a devoted father, a true Christian and a respected citizen.

Second, That we tender to the family of the deceased our heartfelt sympathy.

Third, That the LaRue County Herald be requested to publish the proceedings of this meeting, and a copy of these rsolutions be furnished the family of the deceased, and that the same be spread upon the records of the County and Circuit Courts for LaRue County.

W. H. HAMILTON, Chairman. G. W. THURMAN, Secretary.

At a meeting of B. R. Young Lodge, No. 132, F. & A. M., Hodgenville, Ky., May 20, 1885, the following resolutions were passed, to wit:

WHEREAS, It hath pleased Almighty God to call from our midst, our true and faithful brother, J. F. Cessna. Therefore, be it

RESOLVED, First, That we deplore his loss, but recognizing the fact that he has been called to a higher and more glorious sphere by the

112   THE HOUSE OF CESSNA.

Supreme Architect c' the universe, we bow with reverence, humility and sorrow to the divine decree.

Second, That we tender to the family of the deceased our heartfelt sympathy and condolence.

Third, That a copy of these resolutions be furnished the LaRue County Herald for publication, and a copy be furnished the family of the deceased.
            G. W. THURMAN, J. R. NANTZ, F. M. ROOF, Committee.

TO THE MEMORY OF JUDGE J. F. CESSNA, BY HIS FRIEND, J. TOL. MILLER:

My very heart was pained last Sunday evening as I read in the LaRue County Herald of the death of J. F. Cessna. Far back in memory's path do I remember with pleasure Jonathan Cessna. And whilst perfection is not claimed for him, still he was a great and good man. Great in all the gentle graces that enter into and adorn the gentleman and the Christian, and, when sufficiently aroused, he was eloquently great as an orator upon the rostrum. Though bereft long years ago of a loving wife, he well succeeded in raising their children. The oldest son, a minister of the Gospel, as well as an ex-school teacher, commands the respect and esteem of all who know him. The youngest, also a school teacher of more than ordinary ability, deserves the confidence placed in him. Truly, the sons occupy positions in society the most exalted. The three girls are modest, quiet, graceful, cultured and well prepared to act their part in the great drama of human life. Verily, Judge Cessna was a great man. But alas! he is dead! Yet in his children, and a thousand other ways, he still lives. Here I lay down my pencil in sadness for I shall see his face upon earth no more. But upon heaven's altar I lay my benedictions for his children and the many hearts who mourn his death.

Perrin's History of Kentucky has the following regarding Jonathan Cessna:

"Jonathan Cessna was born November 16, 1804; was a farmer and owner of slaves; served as Sheriff, also Judge of his county for twelve years and also practised law. He was one of the prominent citizens of the county; was a leading member of the Baptist church; also of the Masonic fraternity and died May 19, 1885. He was a son of William Cessna, who married a Miss Wallace, and came from Pennsylvania when a child of four years with his father, who first landed at Louisville, and shortly after settled on Nolin Creek and

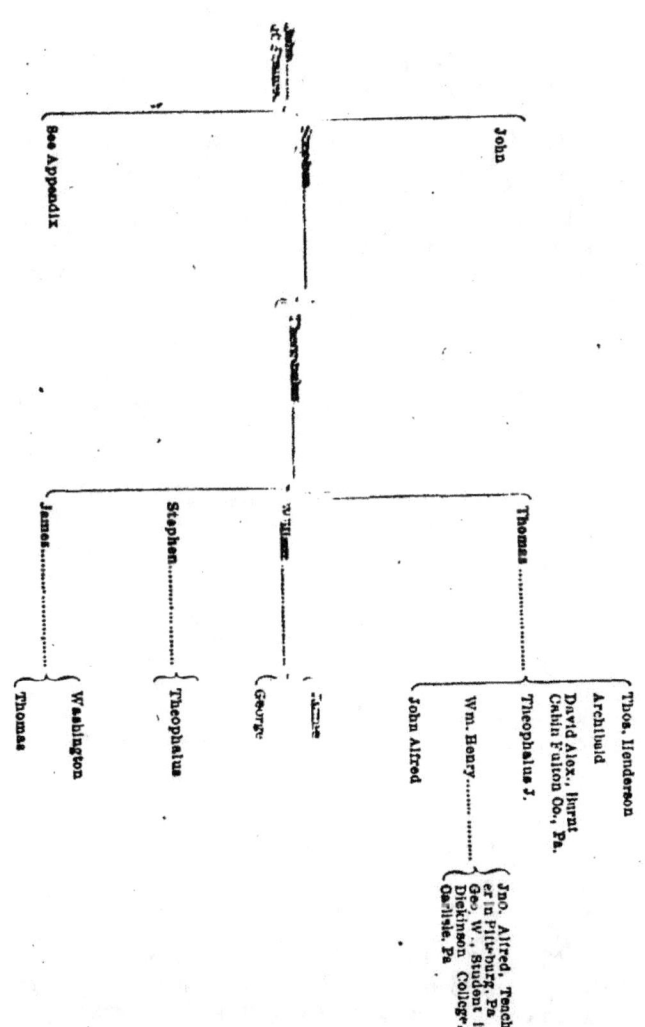

was one of the very early settlers in LaRue County, then Hardin. He was of French descent, his wife coming from Scotland with her parents and settling in LaRue County." Page 952.

In addition to above facts the LaRue County Herald, Hodgensville, Ky., of date May 20, 1885, has the following: "Early in life he began the study of law, was admitted to the bar at this place, and won an enviable reputation as an attorney. His talents appeared to best advantage in land suits, and it is doubtful if there is a member of this bar left whose knowledge of old land claims and the law pertaining to them even approximates that possessed by Judge Cessna. In 1872 he was nominated by the Democracy as their candidate for State Senator but owing to dissaffection in his party was defeated. He was an unwavering Democrat in politics."

AN ACT OF KINDNESS

At the time of Abraham Lincoln's birth his father was away from home. Some of Mrs. Lincoln's neighbors who were with her at the event learned that she was destitute of anything in the nature of food. Some of the ladies called upon Judge William Cessna (IV), one of the most prominent men of that time in this section, in Mrs. Lincoln's behalf, and he donated flour and other articles of food.— Copied from McClure's Magazine of November, 1895, Volume 5, No. 6.

BIOGRAPHY OF THEOPHALUS CISNA

Theophalus Cisna was ensign in Fifth Company, Sixth Battalion of the Pennsylvania soldiers in war of Revolution. Pa. Archives, Vol. 14, page 465.

Theophalus Cisney moved from the upper Tuscarora Valley some place along Jack's Mountains and died there a good deal over one hundred years old. He was the father of six children. viz: James, Thomas, William, Stephen, Betsy and Agnes.

James and Thomas bought land near where they were born, and lived and died there. William and Stephen went west and located about Cincinnati, Ohio. Stephen died there. William came back where he was born and died a good many years ago. Betsy moved some place along the Juniata River. Agnes married and moved to California during the gold excitement in 1848.—From letter of A. S. Cisney January 1, 1897.

Theophalus Cisney. III, John, II, John, I.

Married (1) Miss Richardson. Issue. (1) Betsy, (2) Thomas, (3) James, (4) Stephen, (5) William, (6) Martha. Married (2) Miss Arters. No issue.

BETSY CISNEY IV THEOPHALUS III.

Married John French. Issue: (1) William ,(2) Samuel, (3) Andy, (4) Alexander. Address, Tell township, Huntingdon County, Pa.

JAMES CISNEY IV, THEOPHALUS III.

Married, ——— ———. Issue: (1) Washington, (2) Thomas, (3) Sarah, (4) Margery, (5) Diana, (6) Rachel.

WASHINGTON CISNEY V, JAMES IV.

Married Miss Yocum.

THOMAS CISNEY V JAMES IV,

SARAH CISNEY V, JAMES IV.

Married Robert Parsons.

164

MARGERY CISNEY V.

Married Mr. Butler.

DIANA CISNEY V.

Married Mr. Alexander Hockenberry.

RACHEL CISNEY V.

Married Mr. Kimberland.

STEPHEN CISNEY IV, THEOPHALUS III.

Had one son, Theophalus.

WILLIAM CISNEY IV, THEOPHALUS III.

Married (1) Miss Hogle. Issue: (1) James, (2) George, (3) Margaret.

THOMAS CISNEY IV, THEOPHALUS III.

Born June 14, 1808, died November 10, 1882. Married to Sarah Gifford by Rev. George Gray on August 29, 1833. Issue: Archibald, born June 2, 1834; David Alexander, born January 22, 1836; Theophalus James, born January 27, 1838; Margaret E., born October 4, 1842; William Henry, born March 6, 1846. Arabella, born March 7, 1848. Thomas Henderson, born December 16, 1849; John Alfred, born September 23, 1854.

ARCHIBALD CISNEY V, THOMAS IV,

Married Annie Shin. Issue: Alvilda.

DAVID A. CISNEY V, THOMAS IV.

Lived at Burnt Cabins, Fulton County, Pa. Died April 28, 1892, aged 56 years. Issue: One son and three daughters, one of whom is Rilla.

WILLIAM H. CESSNA V. THOMAS IV.

Married Maggie Kelly. Issue: (1) Sarah Jane, who married Sharswood Parson, a groceryman of Mt. Jenett, McKean County, Pa. (2) John Alfred, a teacher in Pittsburg, Pa. (3) George W., a student at Dickinson College, Carlisle, Pa.

THE CESSNAS OF ADA, OHIO.

From letters received from John Davis Cessna, of Ada, Ohio, it appears that a cousin of John (I) came from France to this country, who was also named John. He was born in 1692 and lived and died in Cumberland County, Pa. He died at the age of 107. His sons were William, John and James—the last two named were never married—and his daughters were Polly, Betsy, Sally and Peggy. William who was born in 1774 and died in 1856, was the father of the following children: (1) John, (2) James, (3) William, (4) George, (5) Joseph, (6) Zackeus, (7) Mary Ann, who married Mr. Wilson.

John D. Cessna, son of William and grandson of John above referred to as having been born in 1692, was born February 2, 1823. Address, Ada, Ohio. Married (1) Eliza Reed. Issue: (1) William Manley, (2) Jackson Phillips, (3) Mary Elizabeth, (4) Albert C., (5) George Henry, (6) John David, (7) Hattie Ann. Married (2) Lyda Ann Obenour. Issue: (1) Bessie Carrie, (2) Meredith Merrill, (3) Clyde Chester.

WILLIAM CESSNA III, WILLIAM II, JOHN I.

Was born November 7, 1852. Married Clara Belle Davis. Issue: (1) Ray, (2) Gail, (3) Gwen, (4) Mary, (5) Hattie. Address, Forest, Ohio.

GEORGE HENRY, (Father of John D., of Ada, Ohio.) Born June 30, 1862. Address, Rosedale, Kansas. Occupation, grain inspector. Married Ann Stewart, a relation of Mary, Queen of Scotland. Issue: Della Bird.

THE END

166

THE HOUSE OF CESSNA.

ANNOUNCEMENT

The author assumes the liberty to appoint the herein-after named descendants as a committee to compile short biographical sketches of their immediate relatives from the present generation back to the fourth generation, to secure photos, to arrange for a family reunion at the St. Louis Fair next year if they so desire, and, in short, formulate any movement of interest to the Cessnas that might suggest itself. About 200 letters properly distributed will acquaint nearly all the Cessnas of the present generation of any movement contemplated. The information collected can be retained by the different members of the committee until a more complete book as refer-

COMMITTEE

Descendants of Jonathan (IV), Rev. Orange Cessna, Ames, Ia.; Prof. W. G. Cisne, Fairfield, Ill.

Descendants of William (IV), Prof. John H. Cessna, Altoona, Pa.; O. J. Cessna, Battle Creek, Mich.; P. A. Cessna, Rosedale, Kan.

Descendants of John (IV), Mrs. Etta Doty, Bedford, Pa.; H. B. Cessna, Bedford, Pa.; John T. Cessna, Grinnel, Ia.; Reon Cessna, Hastings, Neb.

Descendants of Stephen (IV), Dr. W. R. Cisna, Chicago, Ill.

Descendants of Evan and Charles (IV), M. E. Cessna, Hortons, Pa.; G. W. Cessna, Hortons, Pa.

Descendants of Squire James (IV), Roy Cessna, Bedford, Pa.

Descendants of Jonathan (III), of Kentucky, W. C. Cessna, Hodgensville, Ky.; W. C. Durham, Hodgensville, Ky.

Descendants of Stephen (III), of Chillocothe, Ohio, Miss S. F. Cissna, Watseka, Ill.

Where two or more are appointed as a committee in the same line of descent, they can arrange their share of the work agreeably to themselves.

INDEX

Only the names of the male members of the House of Cessna of the present generation, with a few exceptions, is here given. Female members and any male member not herein mentioned can readily trace their lineage by referring to name of their brother, father, or uncle. Preceding the names, date of birth, etc., of the Cessnas will appear an outline showing the line of descent John Cessna I.

Names are given according to State in which members of present generation now live or are prominently identified.

PENNSYLVANIA

ILLINOIS.

	Outline. Page.	Names, Etc. Page.
Dr. W. R. Cisna, Chicago	58	58
William Cissna, Cissna Park	100	103
Stephen Cissna, Watseka	100	103
George King Cissna, Watseka	100	103
Sarah Frances Cissna, Watseka	100	104
Levi M. Cisne, Cisne	100	103
William H. Cisne, Cisne	61	69
Jonah G. Cisne, Cisne	61	69
Charles W. Cessna, Decatur	61	70
Emanuel Cisne, Cisne	94	95
Mrs. Sarah (Cisne) Walters, Fairfield	61	69
T. Benton Cessna, Sumner	61	71
Garfield Cessna, Sumner	61	65
Charles E. Cessna, Chicago	61	66
Lemuel E. Cessna, Fithian	61	76
John Cessna, Hope	61	76

IOWA.

J. Wilson Cessna, Nevada	61	62
Dewitt Cessna, Nevada	61	62
Rev. O. H. Cessna, Ames	61	62
Henry J. Cessna, Smithland	61	72
William A. Cessna, Iowa City	61	72
Clarence Anson Cessna, Iowa City	61	72
Charles Wesley Cessna, Marcus	61	72
Thomas Ceasna, Grinnell	25	33
Newton Cessna, Grinnell	25	34
John T. Cessna, Grinnell	25	34
W. Brown Cessna, Council Bluffs	25	37
Maria Hammer, Iowa City		38
Mrs. Margaret Reno, Iowa City		40
Oliver Cessna, Iowa Falls	61	75
Theodore Cessna, Grinnell	25	27
James A. Jackson, Sioux City		25 and 40

NEBRASKA.

J. Boone Cessna, Hastings	25	37
William Cessna, Grand Island	81	86
Randolph Cessna, Fulton	61	75
Reon B. Cessna, Hastings	25	37

MISSOURI.

Perry Amos Cessna, Sedalia	81	84
William Cessna, Macon	81	86
Charles Cessna, Chillocothe	61	74
Georgia King Cessna, Kansas City	100	104

SOUTH DAKOTA.

William Cessna, Rapid City	61	64
Edward Cessna, Deadwood	61	64
James Cessna, Keystone	61	65

COLORADO.

Ledrue R. Cessna, Cripple Creek	81	89
J. P. Cessna, Clark	94	95

MARYLAND.

Perry Cessna, Mt. Savage	81	91
John K. Cessna, Mt. Savage	81	92
John Calvin Cessna, Cumberland	81	86
William Cessna, Ellerslie	81	86
Thomas H. Cessna, Ellerslie	81	91